JADEN CROSS

Deep Learning Fundamentals with Python

Contents

Deep Learning Basics and Concepts

What is Deep Learning?

Deep learning is a subset of artificial intelligence (AI) and machine learning (ML) that focuses on using complex neural networks to analyze and learn from large datasets. It involves models that imitate the human brain's structure and function, with networks made up of numerous interconnected layers (hence the term "deep") that allow the system to learn patterns and representations from data autonomously. Unlike traditional machine learning, which often relies on manually crafted features and simpler algorithms, deep learning can automatically uncover intricate features and hierarchies in data by adjusting internal parameters through a process known as backpropagation. This gives deep learning models a unique advantage: the ability to identify patterns or correlations in raw data without extensive preprocessing or feature engineering.

The primary objective of deep learning is to enable computers to perform tasks that typically require human intelligence, such as image and speech recognition, language processing, and decision-making. By processing data in layers, deep learning models can transform raw input into increasingly complex representations, allowing them to make accurate predictions, recognize objects, generate text, translate languages, and much more. This capacity has made deep learning instrumental in advancing numerous fields, from natural language processing and computer vision to biomedical sciences and autonomous driving.

At its core, deep learning relies on neural networks, particularly those with many layers—commonly called deep neural networks. These networks consist of "neurons" that process and transmit information across layers. Each neuron receives an input, processes it with an associated weight and bias, applies an activation function to determine if the neuron should activate, and then passes it on to subsequent neurons in the next layer. By adjusting weights and biases through training, the network fine-tunes its predictions, eventually learning to perform complex tasks with minimal human intervention.

The History of Deep Learning

The journey of deep learning dates back to the 1940s, though its widespread adoption and practical success only emerged in recent years. Below is a brief look at its historical evolution:

1. **Early Beginnings (1940s–1960s)**: The foundational idea of artificial neurons was proposed in the 1940s by Warren McCulloch and Walter Pitts, who introduced a mathematical model of neural networks that aimed to simulate how neurons in the human brain process information. In 1958, Frank Rosenblatt developed the perceptron algorithm, an early form of neural network, which showed promise in simple binary classification tasks. However, limitations in processing power and algorithmic shortcomings prevented these early networks from solving more complex problems.

2. **Neural Network Winter (1970s–1980s)**: Neural network research faced significant challenges during this period, known as the "AI winter." Minsky and Papert's influential book, *Perceptrons*, demonstrated the limits of simple perceptrons and highlighted their inability to solve even basic problems, like the XOR function, without multiple layers. As a result, research in neural networks lost momentum, and interest shifted towards other areas of AI.

3. **Backpropagation and Renewed Interest (1980s–1990s)**: In the 1980s, the development of the backpropagation algorithm revived interest in neural networks. Introduced by researchers such as Geoffrey Hinton, David Rumelhart, and Ronald J. Williams, backpropagation

allowed networks to "learn" by adjusting weights based on errors, thus enabling multi-layer neural networks to be trained effectively. This period saw early applications in areas like speech and handwriting recognition, but computational limitations and data scarcity restricted widespread adoption.

4. **Early 2000s–2010: Advances in Hardware and Data Availability**: As computing power improved with the rise of GPUs (Graphics Processing Units), deep learning began to achieve practical success. The proliferation of digital data and the development of large-scale datasets provided the "fuel" required to train deep networks. Pioneers like Yann LeCun, Yoshua Bengio, and Geoffrey Hinton, often referred to as the "godfathers of deep learning," demonstrated that deep networks could excel in tasks such as handwritten digit classification and speech recognition.

5. **2012–Present: The Deep Learning Boom**: The breakthrough moment for deep learning came in 2012, when Alex Krizhevsky, working with Geoffrey Hinton, developed a deep convolutional neural network (CNN) model called AlexNet. This model achieved unprecedented success on the ImageNet Large Scale Visual Recognition Challenge, reducing error rates significantly. AlexNet's success ignited a surge in deep learning research and investment. In the years following, deep learning models achieved state-of-the-art results across various domains, leading to practical applications in self-driving cars, virtual assistants, language translation, healthcare diagnostics, and more.

Today, deep learning continues to be one of the fastest-growing fields in AI, driven by advancements in hardware (e.g., GPUs, TPUs), the availability of massive datasets, and innovations in model architectures, such as transformers and generative adversarial networks (GANs). This journey, from theoretical concepts in the mid-20th century to the practical applications we see today, underscores the transformative potential of deep learning.

The Difference Between Deep Learning and Machine Learning

While deep learning is a subset of machine learning, it is distinct in several important ways. Understanding these differences helps clarify why deep learning has enabled breakthroughs in AI that were previously unattainable with traditional machine learning approaches.

Feature Engineering:

- *Machine Learning*: In traditional machine learning, feature engineering is a crucial step. Domain experts often need to preprocess data and extract features manually to make the data compatible with specific algorithms. For instance, in image recognition, experts might need to identify edges, textures, or colors as features before training a model.
- *Deep Learning*: Deep learning reduces the need for manual feature engineering by automatically extracting complex features from raw data. Through layered representations, a deep learning model can identify patterns and build abstract representations without human intervention. For instance, in image processing, a deep neural network can learn to recognize edges, shapes, and even complex structures without predefined feature extraction.

Model Complexity and Architecture:

- *Machine Learning*: Machine learning algorithms, like decision trees, support vector machines (SVMs), and logistic regression, are generally simpler compared to deep learning architectures. They are often limited in handling complex data and may require tuning through hyperparameters for optimal performance.
- *Deep Learning*: Deep learning models rely on deep neural networks, which consist of multiple hidden layers that increase the model's ability to capture complex patterns. Advanced architectures like convolutional neural networks (CNNs) for image processing, recurrent neural networks (RNNs) for sequence data, and transformers for language processing add flexibility and power to deep learning models.

Data Requirements:

- *Machine Learning*: Traditional machine learning models are usually effective with smaller datasets, as they are often simpler and less prone to overfitting with limited data. In fact, too much data can sometimes slow down the learning process without significantly improving model accuracy.
- *Deep Learning*: Deep learning requires vast amounts of data for training to achieve meaningful accuracy. The hierarchical nature of deep networks, with numerous parameters to learn, makes large datasets essential for training. This data requirement, once a limitation, is now feasible with modern data collection and storage capabilities.

Training Time and Computational Power:

- *Machine Learning*: Machine learning algorithms are generally less computationally demanding and often train more quickly, especially on standard CPUs. They are suitable for tasks where speed and efficiency are more critical than complex data representation.
- *Deep Learning*: Deep learning models are computationally intensive, requiring high-performance hardware such as GPUs or TPUs (Tensor Processing Units). Training deep networks can take hours, days, or even weeks, depending on the model complexity and dataset size. However, recent advances in hardware have made it more feasible to train deep learning models in a reasonable timeframe.

Performance and Applications:

- *Machine Learning*: Traditional machine learning models perform well on structured data and straightforward tasks, such as predictive analytics, classification, and regression on tabular data. For tasks like predicting customer churn, detecting credit card fraud, or estimating house prices, machine learning models can achieve satisfactory results.

- *Deep Learning*: Deep learning shines in tasks involving unstructured data, such as images, text, and audio, where high levels of abstraction and complex pattern recognition are necessary. It has become the gold standard in fields like computer vision, natural language processing, and speech recognition. Applications include autonomous driving, real-time language translation, facial recognition, and even creative tasks like image synthesis and text generation.

In summary, while machine learning and deep learning both fall under the broader AI umbrella, deep learning's layered architecture and ability to process unstructured data have enabled it to outperform traditional machine learning methods in numerous complex domains. As deep learning continues to evolve, it is expected to broaden the scope and sophistication of what AI systems can achieve.

The Landscape of AI, Machine Learning, and Deep Learning: Clarifying Their Relationships

Artificial Intelligence (AI), Machine Learning (ML), and Deep Learning (DL) represent interconnected fields within the domain of intelligent systems. While often used interchangeably in popular media, these terms describe distinct concepts, each building on the others in a hierarchical relationship. Understanding how these terms relate clarifies their specific roles and limitations, helping us appreciate the unique contributions of deep learning within the broader AI landscape.

Artificial Intelligence (AI): The Broad Field of Intelligent Systems

AI is the overarching concept that encompasses any system designed to perform tasks typically requiring human intelligence. These tasks include decision-making, visual perception, speech recognition, language translation, and problem-solving. AI's goal is to create machines that simulate human-like cognitive abilities, enabling them to learn, reason, and adapt over time.

AI can be divided into two main categories:

1. **Narrow AI (Weak AI)**: This type of AI is specialized and focuses on per-forming a single task or a narrow range of tasks effectively. Examples include virtual assistants (like Siri or Alexa), recommendation systems, and facial recognition software. While these systems can outperform humans in specific functions, they lack general intelligence and are not capable of performing outside their designated scope.

2. **General AI (Strong AI)**: General AI refers to a more advanced form of AI that can understand, learn, and apply intelligence to a wide range of tasks, much like a human. It would possess self-awareness, reasoning abilities, and common sense, enabling it to handle tasks across different domains without human intervention. General AI remains theoretical and is a long-term goal in AI research.

AI includes any approach that enables machines to perform intelligent tasks, whether using rule-based systems, statistical methods, or neural networks. Therefore, machine learning and deep learning are subsets of AI, providing specific methods to achieve AI's broader goals.

Machine Learning (ML): Enabling Machines to Learn from Data

Machine learning is a subset of AI focused on teaching machines to learn from experience and make decisions without being explicitly programmed for each task. In ML, a model is trained on historical data and then applies what it learns to make predictions or classifications. Unlike traditional programming, where specific instructions are given to achieve a task, ML models discover patterns in data and improve performance as they are exposed to more data.

Machine learning relies on a variety of algorithms, categorized into three main types:

1. **Supervised Learning**: In supervised learning, the model is trained on a labeled dataset, meaning each data point has input-output pairs (e.g., an image labeled as "cat" or "dog"). The algorithm learns to map inputs to outputs by minimizing the error between predicted and actual

values. Examples include regression and classification tasks, such as predicting house prices or identifying spam emails.

2. **Unsupervised Learning**: Unsupervised learning involves training a model on data without labeled responses. Instead, the algorithm identifies patterns, groupings, or structures in the data. Common unsupervised learning techniques include clustering (e.g., segmenting customers based on purchasing behavior) and dimensionality reduction (e.g., reducing the number of variables in a dataset for visualization).

3. **Reinforcement Learning**: In reinforcement learning, an agent learns to make decisions by interacting with an environment and receiving feedback through rewards or penalties. This type of learning is useful for tasks where a sequence of actions is required to achieve a goal, such as training a robot to navigate a maze or teaching a model to play games like chess or Go.

Machine learning focuses on algorithms that can learn from data, generalizing from examples to make predictions about new data points. This makes it valuable for applications like predictive analytics, natural language processing, and image recognition. However, traditional machine learning methods often rely on human-defined features, requiring significant domain expertise to preprocess data and design feature sets. This is where deep learning distinguishes itself.

Deep Learning (DL): The Power of Neural Networks in AI

Deep learning is a specialized subfield within machine learning that uses artificial neural networks to process and learn from vast amounts of unstructured data. The term "deep" refers to the multiple layers in these neural networks, enabling them to learn hierarchical representations of data. Each layer captures increasingly complex features, allowing the model to understand abstract patterns without manual feature engineering.

In deep learning, a neural network is typically composed of an input layer, multiple hidden layers, and an output layer. Each neuron in a layer receives input from the previous layer, processes it with an activation function, and passes it on to the next layer. Through this multi-layered approach, deep learning models can capture intricate relationships within data, making them highly effective for complex tasks like image classification, language processing, and speech recognition.

Key attributes of deep learning include:

- **Automatic Feature Extraction**: Deep learning models automatically learn useful features from raw data, eliminating the need for manual feature engineering. This makes DL particularly effective for complex, high-dimensional data like images, audio, and text.
- **Scalability with Data and Computational Power**: Deep learning models require large amounts of labeled data and substantial computational resources for training. Advances in hardware (e.g., GPUs, TPUs) have made it feasible to train deep networks, leading to significant improvements in fields such as computer vision and natural language processing.
- **Hierarchical Learning**: By stacking multiple layers, deep learning models can learn representations at different levels of abstraction. For instance, in an image recognition task, initial layers might detect edges, intermediate layers may identify shapes, and deeper layers could recognize complex objects.

Deep learning has become the backbone of modern AI applications that involve unstructured data, making it the primary method for tasks like language modeling (e.g., GPT, BERT), image generation (e.g., GANs), and real-time object detection.

How AI, Machine Learning, and Deep Learning Work Together

AI, ML, and DL exist within a layered hierarchy:

- **AI** is the broadest concept, referring to any computer system capable of performing tasks that normally require human intelligence.
- **Machine Learning** is a subset of AI focused on building models that

can learn from data.

- **Deep Learning** is a subset of machine learning that uses multi-layered neural networks to learn complex representations from large, unstructured datasets.

Here's a breakdown of how these fields interact:

1. **AI as the Ultimate Goal**: AI aims to create machines that exhibit intelligence across a range of tasks, encompassing both narrow and general applications. AI includes various methods, some rule-based and others learning-based.
2. **Machine Learning as a Tool for AI**: Machine learning provides algorithms that allow AI systems to learn from data rather than relying solely on hard-coded rules. This adaptability enables AI to perform better on a wider range of tasks, as ML models can generalize from historical examples to make accurate predictions about new data.
3. **Deep Learning as an Advanced Form of ML**: Deep learning enhances machine learning capabilities by allowing systems to process unstructured data at an unprecedented scale and accuracy. Unlike traditional ML, which often requires human-defined features, DL models learn features automatically, making them more effective for tasks like image and speech recognition where manual feature extraction would be impractical.

Practical Implications of the AI, ML, and DL Relationship

The layered relationship among AI, ML, and DL has practical implications in terms of performance, application, and development:

- **AI Applications Without Learning**: Some AI systems rely on rule-based approaches, such as expert systems used in diagnostics or financial services. While these systems perform well in narrow domains, they lack the flexibility of learning-based approaches and are limited by their rigid rules.

- **Machine Learning's Breadth and Flexibility**: Machine learning models offer more flexibility than rule-based AI, as they can adapt to new data without being explicitly programmed for each scenario. This makes ML a practical choice for applications in predictive modeling, recommendation systems, and fraud detection.
- **Deep Learning's Specialized Power**: Deep learning, with its layered neural networks, has unlocked new possibilities for handling complex, high-dimensional data. For instance, DL models can recognize faces in images, translate text between languages, and even generate human-like text—all tasks that traditional ML struggles to accomplish without substantial preprocessing and feature engineering.

AI, ML, and DL represent different layers of intelligence, each building on the strengths of the previous. AI provides the broad goal of creating intelligent systems, machine learning offers adaptive algorithms that learn from data, and deep learning enables the automatic extraction of complex features. Together, they form a powerful hierarchy that has transformed technology and unlocked unprecedented opportunities in fields like healthcare, finance, manufacturing, and autonomous systems.

By understanding these relationships, it becomes clear why deep learning has revolutionized the AI landscape, enabling breakthroughs that bring us closer to achieving true artificial intelligence.

Common Deep Learning Applications: Brief Case Studies in Key Fields

Deep learning's capacity to analyze vast amounts of unstructured data has made it indispensable across a range of industries, where it addresses complex challenges that traditional algorithms struggle to solve. Here, we explore several fields where deep learning has led to groundbreaking advancements, providing a glimpse into how this technology is transforming various sectors.

Healthcare: Precision Diagnostics and Drug Discovery
Case Study: Medical Imaging and Diagnostics

Deep learning has transformed medical imaging, providing tools that assist radiologists in diagnosing diseases with unprecedented accuracy. Convolutional neural networks (CNNs), in particular, are used extensively in medical imaging to detect abnormalities in X-rays, CT scans, MRIs, and ultrasound images. For instance, CNNs trained on large datasets of labeled images can identify tumors in mammograms, lesions in MRIs, or abnormalities in retinal scans.

- **Example Application**: In breast cancer screening, CNN models are trained to recognize patterns in mammograms that may indicate early signs of cancer. These models perform at or above the level of experienced radiologists, helping to reduce diagnostic errors and enabling faster, more accurate detection. Additionally, by prioritizing cases that need urgent attention, AI systems streamline workflows in high-demand healthcare environments.

Case Study: Drug Discovery and Development

Traditional drug discovery is costly and time-consuming, with new drugs typically taking over a decade to develop. Deep learning accelerates this process by predicting how different compounds will interact with biological targets, thus streamlining preclinical phases of drug research. Techniques such as deep generative models and reinforcement learning allow AI to explore potential chemical compounds and predict their properties, significantly reducing the need for exhaustive lab experimentation.

- **Example Application**: Companies like DeepMind and Insilico Medicine are using deep learning models to generate novel chemical compounds and predict their therapeutic effects. These AI-driven approaches have yielded promising candidates for diseases that have resisted conventional treatment methods, including rare cancers and neurodegenerative disorders.

Finance: Fraud Detection and Algorithmic Trading
Case Study: Fraud Detection

In the financial sector, fraud detection is a critical application where deep learning has made a considerable impact. By training recurrent neural networks (RNNs) or long short-term memory (LSTM) networks on transaction data, AI models can identify suspicious patterns in real-time, detecting and flagging potentially fraudulent activities that conventional methods might miss. The advantage of deep learning in fraud detection lies in its ability to analyze complex sequences of actions and adapt to evolving fraud patterns.

- **Example Application**: Financial institutions like PayPal and Visa use deep learning models to monitor transaction streams and detect anomalies indicative of fraud. These models can learn the spending habits of individual customers, identifying deviations that may signal unauthorized transactions. As a result, fraud detection systems powered by AI have contributed to significantly reducing financial losses and enhancing security for users.

Case Study: Algorithmic Trading

Algorithmic trading relies on automated trading strategies that execute high-speed transactions based on market conditions. Deep learning models provide an edge by analyzing historical data, identifying profitable patterns, and adapting trading strategies in response to changing market trends. This allows financial firms to maximize returns while minimizing risks.

- **Example Application**: Hedge funds and investment banks deploy deep reinforcement learning models to analyze and predict stock price movements, enabling high-frequency trading. These models adapt to real-time financial data, exploiting short-term market inefficiencies to optimize trades. For instance, the use of recurrent neural networks in trading platforms allows models to track temporal dependencies in stock prices, facilitating better predictions of future price changes.

Robotics: Autonomous Navigation and Manipulation
Case Study: Autonomous Vehicles

Deep learning has been instrumental in developing autonomous driving systems, enabling vehicles to perceive, interpret, and navigate complex environments. Computer vision algorithms, especially CNNs, allow self-driving cars to detect and classify objects like pedestrians, traffic lights, and road signs. Deep reinforcement learning further helps autonomous systems make real-time driving decisions.

- **Example Application**: Companies like Tesla, Waymo, and Nvidia use deep learning to power computer vision and decision-making in autonomous vehicles. CNN-based models process real-time camera feeds to identify objects on the road, while reinforcement learning algorithms help the vehicle adapt its behavior based on changing traffic conditions. The integration of LiDAR data with CNN-based image recognition systems enhances object detection capabilities, contributing to safer autonomous navigation.

Case Study: Industrial Robotics

In manufacturing, deep learning enhances robotic systems used for tasks like assembly, sorting, and quality control. For example, deep learning models enable robots to identify, pick, and place objects with precision, especially in scenarios where objects may vary in size, shape, or position. Deep learning-based computer vision systems also enable quality inspection, detecting defects in products more accurately than human workers.

- **Example Application**: In electronics manufacturing, deep learning-powered robots inspect printed circuit boards (PCBs) for defects. CNNs trained on defect-free and defect-containing images identify minute issues, such as soldering errors or misaligned components, that human inspectors might overlook. This reduces defect rates and ensures product quality, enhancing overall manufacturing efficiency.

Natural Language Processing: Language Translation and Sentiment Analysis

Case Study: Real-Time Language Translation

Deep learning has transformed language translation, especially through sequence-to-sequence models and transformer architectures, such as Google's BERT and OpenAI's GPT. By leveraging massive datasets of multilingual text, deep learning models can translate text between languages with remarkable fluency and accuracy. These models capture context and nuances that rule-based translation systems often miss.

- **Example Application**: Google Translate and DeepL use transformer models to provide translations that are contextually accurate, handling even idiomatic expressions and regional dialects. For instance, when translating a sentence from English to Spanish, the model interprets not only individual words but also the overall context, yielding more natural translations.

Case Study: Sentiment Analysis in Customer Feedback

Sentiment analysis, which determines the emotional tone of text, is widely used in applications such as social media monitoring, customer service, and market research. Deep learning models analyze customer reviews, comments, and feedback, categorizing them as positive, negative, or neutral. This helps companies understand customer sentiment and tailor their responses or product offerings accordingly.

- **Example Application**: Businesses like Amazon and Twitter use deep learning for sentiment analysis on customer feedback. By applying recurrent neural networks or transformer-based models, companies extract valuable insights from millions of reviews and social media posts, enabling them to respond to customer issues proactively. This sentiment-driven approach enhances customer satisfaction and improves brand loyalty.

Deep learning's impact across healthcare, finance, robotics, and natural language processing demonstrates its versatility and effectiveness in handling complex data-driven tasks. By leveraging advanced neural network architectures tailored to specific needs, deep learning enables breakthroughs in medical diagnostics, fraud detection, autonomous driving, and language translation, among other applications. As these technologies continue to mature, deep learning's potential to transform industries will only expand, paving the way for further innovation and reshaping the way businesses and societies operate.

Key Concepts in Deep Learning: Neural Networks, Layers, Neurons, Weights, Biases, and Activation Functions

At the heart of deep learning are neural networks, structures inspired by the human brain's functioning. Understanding the foundational components of these networks—neurons, layers, weights, biases, and activation functions—provides insight into how deep learning models process data, make predictions, and learn from mistakes.

Neural Networks: The Building Blocks of Deep Learning

A neural network is a collection of interconnected nodes, or neurons, organized into layers. Each neuron performs a simple computation and passes the result to the next layer of neurons, which process the data further. Neural networks can vary in size and depth, from shallow networks with only a few layers to deep networks with many layers, making them suitable for different levels of complexity in tasks.

The structure of a neural network typically includes three types of layers:

1. **Input Layer**: This is the first layer, where the raw data is fed into the network. Each neuron in this layer represents one feature or attribute of the data, such as the pixels in an image or the words in a sentence.
2. **Hidden Layers**: Located between the input and output layers, hidden layers perform the complex computations needed to transform the input data. The more hidden layers a network has, the "deeper" it is,

which is where the term "deep learning" comes from. Hidden layers extract features from the data, gradually refining and abstracting them with each layer to capture intricate patterns.

3. **Output Layer**: This layer produces the final output, which can be a class label, a probability score, or a predicted value, depending on the task. For example, in an image classification model, the output layer might contain neurons corresponding to each possible class, such as "cat," "dog," or "car."

Each of these layers is a critical component of a neural network, working together to process inputs, extract features, and make predictions or decisions.

Neurons: The Fundamental Units of Neural Networks

Neurons are the primary units of computation in a neural network, similar to biological neurons in the brain. In deep learning, a neuron receives inputs from the previous layer, performs a weighted sum of these inputs, applies an activation function, and sends the result to the next layer. Neurons are organized into layers, with each neuron in a layer connected to every neuron in the next layer.

In a neural network, each neuron represents a single mathematical function, taking inputs from multiple sources, processing them, and passing the output along. For example, in a network classifying handwritten digits, individual neurons might focus on detecting lines, curves, or other features that make up the numbers.

Weights: The Influence of Inputs on Neurons

Weights are essential parameters in a neural network that determine the strength or importance of each input to a neuron. Each connection between neurons has an associated weight, which scales the input value before it's passed through the neuron. During training, the network adjusts these weights to minimize errors and improve accuracy, allowing it to learn the relationships between inputs and outputs.

For example, in a model classifying images of cats and dogs, the weights of neurons in the initial layers may be set to detect basic features, such as edges and textures, which are crucial for distinguishing between the two classes. Over time, the model optimizes these weights to enhance accuracy in identifying the images.

The importance of weights can't be overstated: they encode the "knowledge" learned from the data, guiding the network's decision-making process. Adjusting weights is fundamental to training, as it enables the model to recognize patterns and generalize from examples.

Biases: Enabling Flexibility in Neurons' Responses

Biases are additional parameters in neural networks that adjust the output of neurons independently of the input. Each neuron typically has a bias term that shifts its activation threshold, allowing the model to capture patterns that aren't centered around the origin of the input space. Bias terms give neurons flexibility, enabling them to learn patterns more effectively by controlling the point at which they activate.

Consider a neuron that learns to detect certain patterns in data. Without a bias, the neuron may only activate when a specific weighted sum of inputs is exactly zero. By introducing a bias, the neuron can activate at other values, allowing it to respond to a broader range of patterns.

Biases, like weights, are adjusted during training to minimize error, and they contribute significantly to the model's ability to fit complex data distributions.

Activation Functions: Introducing Non-Linearity

Activation functions are mathematical functions applied to the output of neurons, allowing the network to capture non-linear relationships in the data. Without activation functions, neural networks would behave as linear models, limiting their ability to handle complex tasks. Activation functions introduce non-linearity, enabling the network to approximate intricate mappings between inputs and outputs.

Several activation functions are commonly used in deep learning, each with unique properties suited to different tasks:

1. **Sigmoid Function**: The sigmoid function squashes input values to a range between 0 and 1, making it useful for probabilistic interpretations. However, it suffers from the "vanishing gradient" problem, where gradients become too small in deep networks, hindering learning.

2. **Hyperbolic Tangent (tanh) Function**: Similar to sigmoid, tanh maps inputs to a range between -1 and 1. Tanh is often preferred over sigmoid because it centers the output around zero, which can improve convergence during training.

3. **Rectified Linear Unit (ReLU)**: ReLU is the most widely used activation function in deep learning. It outputs zero for any negative input and returns the input value if it's positive. This simple approach makes ReLU computationally efficient and effective for deep networks. However, ReLU can lead to "dead neurons," where certain neurons permanently output zero if they only receive negative inputs.

4. **Leaky ReLU**: To address the dead neuron problem, Leaky ReLU allows a small, non-zero gradient for negative inputs, enabling neurons to continue learning even with negative inputs.

5. **Softmax Function**: Typically used in the output layer for classification tasks, the softmax function converts raw output scores into probabilities, allowing the network to produce a probability distribution over multiple classes.

Activation functions are critical for enabling neural networks to learn nonlinear patterns in data. By controlling the activation of neurons, these functions allow the network to fit complex data distributions and generalize effectively to new data.

How These Concepts Work Together

In a neural network, each input is multiplied by a weight, adjusted by a bias, and passed through an activation function to produce an output.

Here's how these components interact within a single neuron:

1. **Weighted Sum Calculation**: Each neuron receives multiple inputs from the previous layer. Each input is multiplied by its respective weight, and the results are summed up.
2. $z=\Sigma(wi \cdot xi)+bz = \sum (w\_i \cdot x\_i) + bz=\Sigma(wi \cdot xi)+b$
3. where wiw_iwi represents the weights, xix_ixi the inputs, and bbb the bias term.
4. **Activation**: The weighted sum is passed through an activation function, which introduces non-linearity. This result is then passed to the neurons in the next layer, where the process repeats.
5. $a=f(z)a = f(z)a=f(z)$
6. where fff is the activation function and aaa is the output after activation.

The model adjusts weights and biases throughout training by calculating the error between predicted and actual values and using optimization algorithms (like gradient descent) to minimize this error. This process allows neural networks to "learn" from data, fine-tuning their weights and biases to improve accuracy.

Putting It All Together: An Example

Imagine training a deep learning model to classify images of handwritten digits (as in the popular MNIST dataset). Here's how the components interact to achieve this task:

1. **Input Layer**: Each pixel in the image serves as an input neuron. For a 28x28 pixel image, the input layer would have 784 neurons, each representing a pixel intensity value.
2. **Hidden Layers**: The first hidden layer might detect simple features like edges or contours. As the data progresses through subsequent hidden layers, the network learns more complex features, such as shapes and patterns.
3. **Output Layer**: The output layer has ten neurons, one for each possible

digit (0-9). A softmax activation function assigns probabilities to each neuron, indicating the model's confidence in each classification.

4. **Training Process**: During training, the model iteratively adjusts weights and biases to reduce prediction errors. If the model misclassifies a digit, the weights and biases are updated to minimize the error on the next pass.

Each of these components—neurons, weights, biases, layers, and activation functions—works in concert, enabling the network to learn the complex patterns required for digit classification. As the training progresses, the network improves its accuracy, eventually achieving high precision in recognizing unseen digits.

Neural networks' power lies in their layered structure, flexible weights, adaptable biases, and non-linear activation functions. By combining these elements, deep learning models can tackle complex, high-dimensional data, such as images, audio, and text. Understanding these fundamental concepts is essential for developing and optimizing deep learning applications, as each component plays a critical role in a network's performance, adaptability, and effectiveness.

Essential Deep Learning Terminology: Epochs, Batch Size, Loss Function, and Gradient Descent

To effectively train a deep learning model, it's crucial to understand the terminology and processes that guide model optimization. Here we explore key terms—epochs, batch size, loss function, and gradient descent—that are foundational to building, training, and refining deep learning models.

Epochs: Iterating Over the Data

In deep learning, an **epoch** refers to a single pass through the entire training dataset. When a neural network trains, it adjusts its weights and biases to improve predictions, learning from the errors made in each round. However, because deep learning models need substantial data to generalize well, passing through the data just once is usually insufficient. By processing the data multiple times, the model can better learn patterns, minimize errors, and improve its performance.

Typically, training involves hundreds or thousands of epochs, where each epoch allows the model to see the full dataset once. Through repeated exposure to the data, the model refines its parameters, improving its ability to make accurate predictions. The number of epochs is usually determined experimentally, as setting it too high can lead to overfitting, while setting it too low can result in underfitting.

For example, consider a model training to classify images of animals. During each epoch, the model would see every image in the training dataset and adjust its parameters to better distinguish between different animals (e.g., cats and dogs). After a certain number of epochs, the model ideally learns to classify new images accurately based on its accumulated learning.

Batch Size: Managing Data in Chunks

Batch size refers to the number of samples the model processes before updating its parameters. Instead of processing each sample individually (which is inefficient) or processing the entire dataset in one go (which can be computationally intense), deep learning often uses a middle ground, known as batch processing.

In batch processing:
- A **batch** is a subset of the dataset.
- The **batch size** determines how many samples are in each batch.

Using batches allows the model to update its parameters more frequently than waiting until it processes the entire dataset. This accelerates learning and enables more efficient use of computational resources. Common batch sizes include 32, 64, and 128, but the optimal batch size varies depending on the dataset size and the hardware available.

For instance, if you have a dataset with 10,000 samples and set the batch size to 100, the model will divide the dataset into 100 batches, each containing 100 samples. During each epoch, the model processes each batch independently and updates its parameters based on the aggregated error from that batch. This approach is a compromise between computational efficiency and learning accuracy, providing a balance that often leads to faster training without sacrificing model quality.

Types of Learning Based on Batch Size:

- **Stochastic Gradient Descent (SGD)**: Uses a batch size of one, updating the model parameters after each individual sample. While it can capture detailed information, SGD is computationally expensive and can introduce noise in parameter updates.
- **Mini-Batch Gradient Descent**: Divides the data into mini-batches (e.g., 32, 64 samples) and updates parameters after each batch. This is the most common approach, balancing efficiency with accuracy.
- **Batch Gradient Descent**: Processes the entire dataset in a single batch, updating the parameters only once per epoch. While computationally heavy, it provides stable gradients but can be impractical for large datasets.

Loss Function: Measuring Prediction Error

The **loss function** is a critical component of deep learning that quantifies how well the model's predictions align with the actual results. By calculating the difference between predicted outputs and true values, the loss function provides a measure of error that the model aims to minimize during training. Common loss functions include:

- **Mean Squared Error (MSE)**: Widely used in regression tasks, MSE calculates the square of the difference between predicted and actual values, penalizing larger errors more heavily.
- **Cross-Entropy Loss**: Often used in classification tasks, cross-entropy loss evaluates the probability distribution generated by the model against the actual distribution. By assigning a higher penalty for wrong

predictions, it encourages the model to improve classification accuracy.
- **Binary Cross-Entropy**: A variant of cross-entropy for binary classification tasks, commonly applied in situations where there are only two possible outcomes.

Example: Suppose a model is trained to recognize handwritten digits, predicting "2" for an image of the digit "3." The loss function computes the discrepancy between the prediction and the actual label, generating a loss score. This score provides a guide for updating the model parameters to improve future predictions.

The choice of loss function depends on the problem type (classification or regression), and it significantly influences the model's learning process. By minimizing the loss function, the model gradually learns to make more accurate predictions.

Gradient Descent: Optimizing the Model Parameters

Gradient Descent is the optimization algorithm that underpins the learning process in neural networks. It's a mathematical method used to minimize the loss function by iteratively adjusting the model's parameters (weights and biases) in the direction that reduces error. The gradient refers to the derivative of the loss function with respect to each parameter, providing a direction for adjustment to minimize the error.

Here's how gradient descent works:

1. **Calculate the Loss**: For each batch, the model computes the loss based on its current predictions.
2. **Compute the Gradient**: The model calculates the gradients, which indicate how much each parameter needs to be adjusted to minimize the loss.
3. **Update Parameters**: The parameters are updated by moving in the direction opposite to the gradient (downhill), which reduces the loss. This adjustment is controlled by a factor called the **learning rate**.
4. **Repeat**: The model repeats this process for each batch, gradually

reducing the loss across epochs until it converges to an optimal solution.

Learning Rate: Controlling the Step Size in Gradient Descent

The **learning rate** is a crucial hyperparameter in gradient descent, controlling the size of the steps the model takes when updating parameters. If the learning rate is too high, the model may overshoot the optimal solution, causing it to diverge. Conversely, if the learning rate is too low, the model may take too long to converge, resulting in slower training.

Typically, the learning rate is fine-tuned based on experimentation, and it can be adjusted during training using **learning rate schedules** or **adaptive optimizers** like **Adam** or **RMSprop**. These adaptive optimizers adjust the learning rate dynamically, balancing faster convergence with stability in model updates.

Variants of Gradient Descent

Several variations of gradient descent are commonly used to optimize deep learning models:

1. **Stochastic Gradient Descent (SGD)**: In SGD, the model updates its parameters after every individual sample, making the process noisier but potentially helping to escape local minima in the loss function. It's well-suited for large datasets, though it requires careful tuning of the learning rate to achieve stability.

2. **Mini-Batch Gradient Descent**: Mini-batch gradient descent is the most widely used variant, processing data in small batches rather than one sample or the entire dataset at a time. It balances computational efficiency and stability, reducing noise while maintaining frequent updates.

3. **Momentum-Based Gradient Descent**: Momentum helps the model accelerate in relevant directions while dampening oscillations in others. By adding a fraction of the previous update to the current one, it reduces the effect of minor fluctuations in gradients, speeding up

convergence.

4. **Adam Optimizer**: Adam (Adaptive Moment Estimation) is a widely used optimizer that combines elements of momentum and adaptive learning rates. It adjusts the learning rate for each parameter individually based on its historical gradient values, leading to faster and more stable convergence.

Practical Example: Gradient Descent in Action

Imagine a neural network trained to predict house prices based on features like size, location, and age. During each iteration:

1. The model predicts prices for a batch of houses and calculates the error (loss) by comparing these predictions to actual prices.
2. Using the loss function, the model calculates gradients for each parameter (weight and bias) based on how much each feature impacts the error.
3. The parameters are adjusted in the direction opposite to the gradients to reduce error, with the learning rate controlling the size of each adjustment.

Over time, this iterative process enables the model to better approximate the relationship between house features and prices. By the end of training, the network's weights are optimized to make predictions that closely match actual house prices.

Epochs, batch size, loss functions, and gradient descent are foundational concepts in deep learning, each playing a unique role in model training. Epochs represent the iterations through the dataset, batch size determines how many samples are processed at once, the loss function quantifies prediction errors, and gradient descent optimizes the model by adjusting parameters to minimize those errors. Together, these components enable deep learning models to learn complex patterns in data, improving their predictive accuracy and generalization abilities with each training iteration.

Setting Up Your Python Environment

Installing Python and Jupyter Notebooks: Step-by-Step Setup for **Python, Jupyter, and Necessary Packages**

Setting up a functional and efficient Python environment is essential for any deep learning project. This chapter will guide you through installing Python, Jupyter Notebook, and essential packages necessary for deep learning. Following these steps will ensure that your environment is ready to execute and experiment with code, explore data, and visualize results.

Step 1: Installing Python

Python is the programming language at the core of deep learning workflows. The latest Python versions (3.8 and above) come with improved performance and extended support for libraries. Here's how to install Python on various operating systems.

1.1 Installing Python on Windows
Download the Python Installer:

- Visit the official Python download page and download the latest version of Python for Windows.

Run the Installer:

- Open the downloaded file and select the option to "Add Python to PATH." This is crucial as it allows Python to be accessed globally from any command prompt window.

- Click on "Install Now" and follow the on-screen instructions. The installer will automatically set up Python on your machine.

Verify Installation:

- Open Command Prompt and type python —version to confirm the installation. You should see the installed Python version displayed.

1.2 Installing Python on macOS
Using Homebrew (Recommended):

- Homebrew simplifies the installation process for various software on macOS. If you haven't installed Homebrew, open Terminal and run:

```bash
/bin/bash -c "$(curl -fsSL
https://raw.githubusercontent.com/Homebrew/install/HEAD/install.sh)"
```

Install Python with Homebrew:

- Once Homebrew is installed, run:

```bash
brew install python
```

- This will install the latest Python version and configure the environment path automatically.

Verify Installation:

- In Terminal, type python3 —version to confirm Python is installed correctly.

1.3 Installing Python on Linux

For most Linux distributions, Python comes pre-installed. However, if you need the latest version, follow these steps:

Update the System Package Index:

- Open Terminal and run:

```bash

sudo apt update
```

Install Python:

- Use the package manager to install Python:

```bash

sudo apt install python3
```

Verify Installation:

- Confirm Python installation by running python3 —version in the terminal.

Step 2: Setting Up Jupyter Notebook

Jupyter Notebook is a versatile tool for writing, testing, and documenting code in a single environment. Widely used in data science and machine learning, Jupyter allows for interactive coding, visualizations, and easy-to-read documentation, making it ideal for deep learning workflows.

2.1 Installing Jupyter Notebook Using pip

After installing Python, you can install Jupyter Notebook directly using the pip package manager.

Install pip:

- If pip is not already installed, install it with:

```bash
python -m ensurepip --upgrade
```

Install Jupyter Notebook:

- Run the following command to install Jupyter Notebook:

```bash
pip install notebook
```

Launch Jupyter Notebook:

- Start Jupyter by running:

```bash
jupyter notebook
```

- This command opens a new tab in your default web browser with the Jupyter Notebook interface.

2.2 Installing Jupyter Notebook Using Anaconda (Alternative)

Anaconda simplifies package management and provides an isolated environment for Python development, making it a popular choice for data scientists and machine learning engineers.

Download Anaconda:

- Go to the Anaconda website and download the installer suitable for your operating system.

Run the Installer:

- Follow the on-screen instructions, ensuring to select the option to "Add Anaconda to PATH."

Launch Jupyter Notebook:

- Open Terminal (or Command Prompt on Windows) and type:

```bash

jupyter notebook
```

- Jupyter Notebook will open in your web browser, ready to use.

Step 3: Installing Essential Deep Learning Packages

Once you have Python and Jupyter Notebook installed, the next step is to install the libraries necessary for deep learning. Key libraries include NumPy, pandas, Matplotlib, scikit-learn, TensorFlow, and PyTorch. These libraries support tasks ranging from data manipulation to advanced model building and optimization.

3.1 Installing Libraries with pip

Open a terminal (or Command Prompt) and install each library individually using pip:

NumPy (for numerical computations):

```bash
```

```bash
pip install numpy
```

pandas (for data manipulation and analysis):

```bash
```

```bash
pip install pandas
```

Matplotlib (for data visualization):

```bash
```

```bash
pip install matplotlib
```

scikit-learn (for machine learning algorithms and tools):

```bash
```

```bash
pip install scikit-learn
```

TensorFlow (for deep learning):

```bash
pip install tensorflow
```

PyTorch (alternative deep learning library):

```bash
pip install torch
```

3.2 Installing Libraries with Conda (Anaconda)

If you're using Anaconda, it's often simpler to use conda for package installation, as it manages dependencies more efficiently:

NumPy:

```bash
conda install numpy
```

pandas:

```bash
conda install pandas
```

Matplotlib:

```bash
conda install matplotlib
```

scikit-learn:

```bash
conda install scikit-learn
```

TensorFlow:

```bash
conda install tensorflow
```

PyTorch:

```bash
conda install pytorch torchvision torchaudio -c pytorch
```

Using conda is often more stable, particularly for TensorFlow and PyTorch, as it handles complex dependencies and compatibility issues more efficiently.

Step 4: Setting Up Virtual Environments (Optional but Recommended)

Virtual environments create isolated spaces for different projects, ensuring that library versions don't conflict across projects. This is especially useful when working with deep learning libraries that may require specific versions.

4.1 Creating a Virtual Environment Using venv

The venv module is included in Python 3 and is straightforward to use.

Create a Virtual Environment:

- Open Terminal or Command Prompt, navigate to your project directory, and run:

```bash
python -m venv myenv
```

- Replace "myenv" with your preferred environment name.

Activate the Virtual Environment:

- On Windows:

```bash
myenv\Scripts\activate
```

- On macOS/Linux:

```bash
source myenv/bin/activate
```

Install Packages in the Virtual Environment:

- With the environment active, install packages using pip. For example:

```bash
```

```
pip install numpy pandas matplotlib tensorflow
```

Deactivate the Environment:

- To exit the virtual environment, simply run:

```bash
deactivate
```

4.2 Creating a Virtual Environment Using Conda

If you're using Anaconda, you can create virtual environments with conda.

Create the Environment:

```bash
conda create --name myenv
```

Activate the Environment:

```bash
conda activate myenv
```

Install Packages in the Environment:

- Install packages directly using conda:

```bash
```

```
conda install numpy pandas matplotlib tensorflow
```

Deactivate the Environment:

- To deactivate, simply type:

```
bash
```

```
conda deactivate
```

Using virtual environments keeps dependencies organized and avoids conflicts, especially when handling deep learning libraries with complex versioning requirements.

By following these steps, you've set up Python, Jupyter Notebook, and the essential deep learning libraries. You're now equipped with a stable environment for developing deep learning models, experimenting with data, and refining results interactively. With this environment in place, the upcoming chapters will guide you through hands-on coding, model building, and advanced experimentation, setting the foundation for practical deep learning applications.

Key Libraries Overview: Introduction to NumPy, Pandas, Matplotlib, TensorFlow, Keras, and PyTorch

In deep learning, a set of core libraries underpins everything from basic data manipulation to advanced neural network training. This section explores the primary libraries you'll need: **NumPy**, **Pandas**, **Matplotlib**, **TensorFlow**, **Keras**, and **PyTorch**. Each library has unique strengths that enable efficient data processing, visualization, and model building. Let's look at each of these libraries to understand how they contribute to a deep learning workflow.

NumPy: The Foundation for Numerical Computations

NumPy (Numerical Python) is a fundamental library for scientific computing in Python. It provides support for large, multi-dimensional arrays and matrices, along with an extensive collection of mathematical functions to operate on these arrays. Many deep learning libraries, such as TensorFlow and PyTorch, are built on top of or designed to integrate with NumPy's data structures.

Key Features of NumPy:

- **Arrays and Matrices**: NumPy's ndarray object is faster and more efficient than traditional Python lists, which is essential for handling large datasets in deep learning.
- **Mathematical Operations**: NumPy supports a wide range of mathematical functions, from simple arithmetic to complex linear algebra, Fourier transforms, and random number generation.
- **Broadcasting**: This allows you to perform operations on arrays of different shapes without the need to explicitly resize them, improving code efficiency.

Example Use Case:

In deep learning, NumPy is often used to preprocess data, perform mathematical operations on large datasets, and handle matrix transformations.

```python
python

import numpy as np

# Creating a NumPy array
array = np.array([1, 2, 3, 4, 5])
# Performing mathematical operations
mean = np.mean(array)
standard_deviation = np.std(array)
```

Pandas: Data Manipulation and Analysis

38

Pandas is an essential library for data manipulation, cleaning, and analysis. Built on top of NumPy, Pandas introduces powerful data structures like **DataFrames** and **Series** that simplify working with structured data.

Key Features of Pandas:

- **DataFrames and Series**: The DataFrame is a two-dimensional labeled data structure, similar to a table, while Series is a one-dimensional array with labels.
- **Data Cleaning and Transformation**: Pandas provides tools to handle missing data, merge datasets, and filter data, all of which are crucial for preparing datasets for deep learning.
- **Data Aggregation and Grouping**: Pandas can group data and apply summary functions, making it easier to gain insights from large datasets.

Example Use Case:

In deep learning, Pandas is often used to import, clean, and preprocess datasets before they are fed into a model. For example:

```python
python

import pandas as pd

# Loading a dataset
data = pd.read_csv('data.csv')
# Checking for missing values
missing_data = data.isnull().sum()
# Filling missing values
data.fillna(0, inplace=True)
```

Matplotlib: Visualization and Plotting

Matplotlib is a comprehensive library for creating static, animated, and interactive visualizations in Python. It's the primary tool for data visualization in the Python ecosystem, allowing deep learning practitioners to visualize data trends and model performance.

Key Features of Matplotlib:

- **Plotting Functions**: Matplotlib offers a variety of chart types, such as line, scatter, histogram, and bar plots.
- **Customization**: You can control every aspect of a plot, from colors to axis labels, enabling precise and publication-quality visualizations.
- **Integration with Other Libraries**: Matplotlib integrates well with libraries like Pandas, making it easy to visualize data directly from DataFrames.

Example Use Case:

In deep learning, Matplotlib is used to visualize data distributions, monitor training progress, and evaluate model predictions.

```python
import matplotlib.pyplot as plt

# Plotting a simple line graph
x = [1, 2, 3, 4, 5]
y = [2, 3, 5, 7, 11]
plt.plot(x, y, label="Line plot")
plt.xlabel("X-axis")
plt.ylabel("Y-axis")
plt.legend()
plt.show()
```

TensorFlow: Deep Learning Framework by Google

TensorFlow is an open-source deep learning library developed by Google. It's one of the most widely used deep learning libraries, known for its flexibility, scalability, and support for both research and production environments. TensorFlow is suitable for building and deploying machine learning and deep learning models at scale.

Key Features of TensorFlow:

- **TensorFlow Core**: This provides the essential building blocks for defining and running computational graphs, allowing low-level control over model architecture and training.

- **Keras API**: TensorFlow comes with Keras, a high-level API that simplifies model creation, making it easier for beginners to build deep learning models.
- **TensorBoard**: TensorFlow's visualization toolkit allows you to monitor model performance, track metrics, and visualize complex data structures.
- **Support for Distributed Training**: TensorFlow can be used to train models on large datasets using multiple GPUs or TPUs, making it suitable for industrial-scale deep learning applications.

Example Use Case:

TensorFlow is commonly used for building neural networks for tasks like image classification, text generation, and sequence prediction.

```python
import tensorflow as tf

# Define a simple neural network model
model = tf.keras.Sequential([
    tf.keras.layers.Dense(64, activation='relu'),
    tf.keras.layers.Dense(10, activation='softmax')
])
# Compile the model
model.compile(optimizer='adam',
loss='sparse_categorical_crossentropy', metrics=['accuracy'])
```

Keras: High-Level Deep Learning API

Keras is a user-friendly, high-level API for building and training neural networks. Initially an independent library, Keras is now part of TensorFlow and serves as its official high-level API. Keras abstracts much of the complexity of deep learning, making it accessible to beginners.

Key Features of Keras:

- **Modularity**: Keras is built around key components that are interchangeable, such as layers, loss functions, and optimizers.
- **Ease of Use**: With Keras, it's possible to quickly prototype neural networks with minimal code, making it ideal for experimentation.
- **Seamless Integration with TensorFlow**: As part of TensorFlow, Keras has access to TensorFlow's performance optimizations and deployment capabilities.

Example Use Case:

Keras is ideal for quick prototyping and developing models for structured and unstructured data.

```python
from tensorflow.keras.models import Sequential
from tensorflow.keras.layers import Dense

# Define a simple neural network using Keras
model = Sequential([
    Dense(128, activation='relu', input_shape=(784,)),
    Dense(10, activation='softmax')
])
model.compile(optimizer='adam', loss='categorical_crossentropy',
metrics=['accuracy'])
```

PyTorch: Deep Learning Framework by Facebook

PyTorch is an open-source deep learning library developed by Facebook's AI Research lab. Known for its flexibility and dynamic computation graphs, PyTorch is popular among researchers and developers who want more control over model training and experimentation.

Key Features of PyTorch:

- **Dynamic Computational Graphs**: Unlike TensorFlow's static graphs, PyTorch allows you to define and manipulate computational graphs on the fly, making it more intuitive for debugging and experimentation.

- **Integration with NumPy**: PyTorch's Tensor objects are similar to NumPy arrays, enabling seamless integration with existing scientific computing code.
- **Strong GPU Acceleration**: PyTorch leverages CUDA for fast computations on GPUs, essential for training large models.
- **Torchvision Library**: This library within PyTorch provides datasets, model architectures, and image transformations, making it easier to work with vision-based tasks.

Example Use Case:

PyTorch is widely used in research and academic settings for applications such as natural language processing, computer vision, and reinforcement learning.

```python
import torch
import torch.nn as nn
import torch.optim as optim

# Define a simple model
class SimpleModel(nn.Module):
    def __init__(self):
        super(SimpleModel, self).__init__()
        self.fc1 = nn.Linear(784, 128)
        self.fc2 = nn.Linear(128, 10)

    def forward(self, x):
        x = torch.relu(self.fc1(x))
        x = self.fc2(x)
        return x

# Instantiate and train the model
model = SimpleModel()
optimizer = optim.Adam(model.parameters(), lr=0.001)
```

These libraries — **NumPy, Pandas, Matplotlib, TensorFlow, Keras**, and **PyTorch** — form the backbone of deep learning development in Python. Each plays a unique role in the workflow, from data preprocessing to visualization to model training and deployment. Understanding these libraries will provide a strong foundation as you build, train, and optimize deep learning models throughout this book.

Working with Jupyter Notebooks: Basic Notebook Usage for Data Exploration and Visualization

Jupyter Notebooks have become an indispensable tool for data scientists, machine learning engineers, and deep learning practitioners. The interactive nature of Jupyter Notebooks makes it ideal for exploring data, developing machine learning models, and visualizing results in real-time. In this section, we will explore how to effectively use Jupyter Notebooks for deep learning tasks, from data exploration and preprocessing to creating visualizations.

What is Jupyter Notebooks?

Jupyter Notebooks are web-based interactive computing environments that allow you to create and share documents containing live code, equations, visualizations, and narrative text. The platform supports multiple programming languages, but it's most commonly used with Python, making it highly relevant for deep learning tasks.

Jupyter Notebooks combine code execution with rich text elements, enabling an intuitive workflow where users can write and execute code in small blocks, or "cells", and immediately see the results. This makes the process of iterative testing and debugging extremely efficient, which is crucial when working with complex models.

Installing Jupyter Notebooks

To get started with Jupyter Notebooks, you need to have it installed on your system. If you've already installed **Python** and **Anaconda** (which includes Jupyter), you can skip the installation steps.

Installation via Anaconda (Recommended for Beginners):

Anaconda is a Python distribution that comes with a suite of libraries and tools, including Jupyter Notebooks.

1. **Download Anaconda**: Go to Anaconda's official website and download the installer for your operating system.

2. **Install Anaconda**: Follow the on-screen instructions to complete the installation.

3. **Launch Jupyter Notebooks**: Once Anaconda is installed, open the Anaconda Navigator, and you will find the option to launch Jupyter Notebooks. Alternatively, you can open a terminal or command prompt and type jupyter notebook to start Jupyter.

Installation via pip (For Advanced Users):

If you prefer not to use Anaconda, you can install Jupyter using pip:

```bash

pip install notebook
```

Once installed, you can start Jupyter by running the command:

```bash

jupyter notebook
```

This will launch Jupyter Notebooks in your default web browser.

Basic Usage of Jupyter Notebooks

Once Jupyter Notebooks is up and running, you'll see the main dashboard where you can create new notebooks or open existing ones. Here's a basic rundown of how to use Jupyter Notebooks:

Cells in Jupyter Notebooks

Jupyter Notebooks consist of **cells** where you can write code or text. There are two main types of cells:

- **Code Cells**: This is where you write your Python code. After writing code in a code cell, you can execute it by pressing Shift + Enter or by clicking the "Run" button in the toolbar. The output of the code will be displayed directly below the cell.
- **Markdown Cells**: These are used for writing text, including explanations, mathematical equations (using LaTeX syntax), and other annotations. Markdown allows you to format your text, include headers, bullet points, and embed links.

To create a new cell, click the "+" button in the toolbar. You can switch between code and markdown cells using the dropdown menu in the toolbar or by pressing Esc followed by M for markdown or Y for code.

Running Code and Viewing Output

To run the code inside a cell, press Shift + Enter. This will execute the code, and the output will be displayed right below the cell. This makes it easy to test small snippets of code or run large data processing scripts without leaving the notebook.

```python
# Example Code Cell in Jupyter
import numpy as np

# Creating an array and computing its mean
arr = np.array([1, 2, 3, 4, 5])
mean = np.mean(arr)

mean  # This will output the mean value directly in the cell's output
```

Saving and Sharing Notebooks

Jupyter Notebooks are saved with the .ipynb file extension. You can save your notebook by clicking the **Save** button in the toolbar or using the keyboard shortcut Ctrl + S. You can also share your notebooks by exporting them in various formats such as HTML, PDF, or Python scripts via **File > Download as**.

Data Exploration in Jupyter Notebooks

One of the main uses of Jupyter Notebooks in deep learning is for data exploration and visualization. Data scientists and deep learning practitioners use notebooks to load datasets, inspect them, clean them, and visualize them before feeding them into models.

Loading Data

The most common format for loading data into a Jupyter Notebook is **CSV** (Comma Separated Values). Pandas is often used to read CSV files, as it provides powerful data manipulation functions. For example:

```python
import pandas as pd

# Load a dataset
data = pd.read_csv('data.csv')

# Display the first 5 rows
data.head()
```

Pandas makes it easy to view summary statistics and data types, identify missing values, and clean the dataset before analysis.

Data Inspection

Once the data is loaded, you can inspect it by calling functions such as .head(), .tail(), or .info(). This helps you understand the structure of the data, identify any missing values, and get a sense of its scale and distribution.

```python
python

# Check the data types and non-null counts
data.info()

# Display summary statistics
data.describe()
```

Handling Missing Data

Missing data is common in real-world datasets. Pandas offers several methods to handle missing values, such as:

- **Filling Missing Values**: You can fill missing values with a specific value (e.g., the mean, median, or a constant).

```python
python

data.fillna(data.mean(), inplace=True)
```

- **Dropping Missing Values**: If rows or columns have too many missing values, you might decide to drop them.

```python
python

data.dropna(inplace=True)
```

Visualizing Data

Visualizing data is essential to understanding its underlying structure, trends, and relationships. In Jupyter Notebooks, **Matplotlib** and **Seaborn** are commonly used for creating plots.

- **Line Plots**: Useful for tracking changes over time.

python

```python
import matplotlib.pyplot as plt

plt.plot(data['column_name'])
plt.xlabel('X-axis Label')
plt.ylabel('Y-axis Label')
plt.title('Line Plot Example')
plt.show()
```

- **Histograms**: Useful for understanding the distribution of a dataset.

python

```python
data['column_name'].hist()
plt.title('Histogram Example')
plt.show()
```

- **Scatter Plots**: Useful for visualizing the relationship between two continuous variables.

python

```python
plt.scatter(data['feature1'], data['feature2'])
plt.xlabel('Feature 1')
plt.ylabel('Feature 2')
plt.title('Scatter Plot Example')
plt.show()
```

- **Heatmaps**: Useful for visualizing correlations between features.

```python
import seaborn as sns

sns.heatmap(data.corr(), annot=True, cmap='coolwarm')
plt.title('Correlation Heatmap')
plt.show()
```

These visualizations help you identify patterns in the data and determine how different features relate to each other, aiding in feature selection and engineering.

Building Models in Jupyter Notebooks

As you work through your deep learning projects, Jupyter Notebooks offer an ideal environment for developing and training machine learning and deep learning models. You can:

- Build models using libraries such as **TensorFlow**, **Keras**, and **PyTorch**.
- Train the model on your data and monitor its performance using built-in visualization tools.
- Track metrics and visualize the loss and accuracy during the training process.

Example of building a simple model using **Keras**:

```python
from tensorflow.keras.models import Sequential
from tensorflow.keras.layers import Dense

# Define the model
```

```
model = Sequential([
    Dense(64, activation='relu', input_dim=10),
    Dense(1, activation='sigmoid')
])

# Compile the model
model.compile(optimizer='adam', loss='binary_crossentropy',
metrics=['accuracy'])

# Train the model
history = model.fit(X_train, y_train, epochs=10, batch_size=32)

# Plotting the training history
plt.plot(history.history['accuracy'], label='accuracy')
plt.plot(history.history['loss'], label='loss')
plt.xlabel('Epoch')
plt.ylabel('Value')
plt.legend()
plt.show()
```

This setup allows you to run training cycles and experiment with different architectures while keeping track of the model's progress visually.

Jupyter Notebooks serve as a powerful tool for data exploration, visualization, and model building. They offer an interactive environment that supports real-time coding, immediate feedback, and seamless integration with libraries like **Pandas**, **Matplotlib**, **TensorFlow**, **Keras**, and **PyTorch**. Whether you're cleaning data, visualizing trends, or experimenting with deep learning models, Jupyter provides an ideal platform for developing and documenting your deep learning workflows. As you progress in this book, you'll frequently return to Jupyter Notebooks to experiment with code and refine your models, making it a crucial part of your deep learning toolkit.

Data Handling in Python: Data Preprocessing, Transformation, and Visualization Techniques

Data handling is one of the most crucial steps in any data science or machine learning workflow, including deep learning. Raw data rarely comes in the perfect form to train a deep learning model. It often requires preprocessing, transformation, and visualization to make it suitable for analysis. This section will explore various techniques to handle data effectively using Python, with a particular focus on **data preprocessing**, **data transformation**, and **data visualization**.

Data Preprocessing

Data preprocessing is the process of preparing raw data for analysis by transforming it into a cleaner and more understandable format. This step ensures that the dataset is suitable for training a machine learning or deep learning model.

1. Handling Missing Data

Handling missing data is one of the first and most important tasks in preprocessing. Missing data can lead to biased models, decreased performance, or errors during training. There are several methods for dealing with missing values:

- **Remove Missing Data**: If a feature or a row has too many missing values, it might be best to remove it from the dataset.

python

```python
# Drop rows with missing values
data.dropna(inplace=True)

# Drop columns with too many missing values
data.dropna(axis=1, thresh=int(0.8*len(data)), inplace=True)
```

- **Impute Missing Values**: If removing missing data is not feasible, you can impute missing values with some form of statistical replacement, like the mean, median, or mode.

python

```
# Impute missing values with the mean of the column
data.fillna(data.mean(), inplace=True)

# Impute with the median
data.fillna(data.median(), inplace=True)
```

- **Forward/Backward Fill**: For time-series data or when there is a clear order in data, forward or backward filling can be useful.

python

```
data.fillna(method='ffill', inplace=True)  # Forward fill
data.fillna(method='bfill', inplace=True)  # Backward fill
```

2. Scaling and Normalization

Deep learning models, especially those with gradient-based optimization (like neural networks), perform better when the input data is scaled to a consistent range. Common techniques include:

- **Standardization**: This involves subtracting the mean and dividing by the standard deviation, which centers the data around 0 and scales it to unit variance.

```python
python

from sklearn.preprocessing import StandardScaler

scaler = StandardScaler()
scaled_data = scaler.fit_transform(data)
```

- **Normalization**: Scaling the data so that the values lie between 0 and 1, often using the Min-Max scaling technique.

```python
python

from sklearn.preprocessing import MinMaxScaler

scaler = MinMaxScaler()
normalized_data = scaler.fit_transform(data)
```

- **Robust Scaling**: For datasets with many outliers, **RobustScaler** uses the median and interquartile range (IQR) for scaling, making it more robust to outliers.

```python
python

from sklearn.preprocessing import RobustScaler

scaler = RobustScaler()
scaled_data = scaler.fit_transform(data)
```

3. Encoding Categorical Variables

Deep learning models cannot work directly with categorical data (e.g., labels like "Red", "Blue", "Green"). Therefore, we need to convert categorical variables into numerical values:

- **Label Encoding**: Convert each unique category into a numerical label.

python

```
from sklearn.preprocessing import LabelEncoder

encoder = LabelEncoder()
data['category'] = encoder.fit_transform(data['category'])
```

- **One-Hot Encoding**: For nominal categorical variables (where there is no ordinal relationship between categories), we can create binary columns for each category.

python

```
data = pd.get_dummies(data, columns=['category'])
```

- **Ordinal Encoding**: If the categorical feature has a meaningful order (e.g., "Low", "Medium", "High"), ordinal encoding is preferred.

python

```
from sklearn.preprocessing import OrdinalEncoder

encoder = OrdinalEncoder()
data['category'] = encoder.fit_transform(data[['category']])
```

4. Handling Outliers

Outliers can skew the performance of deep learning models. Identifying and handling outliers is crucial for the quality of your model:

- **Z-Score**: The Z-score is a measure of how many standard deviations a data point is away from the mean. Points that have a Z-score greater than 3 or less than -3 are typically considered outliers.

python

```
from scipy.stats import zscore

data['z_score'] = zscore(data['feature'])
outliers = data[data['z_score'].abs() > 3]
```

- **IQR Method**: The Interquartile Range (IQR) can be used to identify outliers. Data points outside of 1.5 times the IQR are typically considered outliers.

python

```
Q1 = data['feature'].quantile(0.25)
Q3 = data['feature'].quantile(0.75)
IQR = Q3 - Q1

outliers = data[(data['feature'] < (Q1 - 1.5 * IQR)) |
(data['feature'] > (Q3 + 1.5 * IQR))]
```

You can choose to either remove these outliers or replace them with more appropriate values.

Data Transformation

Data transformation is the process of converting raw data into a more appropriate format for analysis. It often involves reshaping, aggregating, or modifying the data to better align with your model's requirements.

1. **Feature Engineering**

Feature engineering is the process of using domain knowledge to create new features from existing data that make machine learning models more effective.

- **Creating Polynomial Features**: By adding polynomial features, such as squared or interaction terms between variables, you can capture more complex relationships in your data.

python

```python
from sklearn.preprocessing import PolynomialFeatures

poly = PolynomialFeatures(degree=2)
poly_features = poly.fit_transform(data[['feature1', 'feature2']])
```

- **Binning**: Grouping continuous data into discrete bins can help with models that do not work well with continuous data.

python

```python
data['age_bin'] = pd.cut(data['age'], bins=[0, 18, 35, 50, 100],
labels=['<18', '18-35', '35-50', '>50'])
```

2. Data Reshaping

Deep learning models often require data in specific shapes, especially for time-series analysis or when dealing with images. Reshaping the data to meet these requirements is common:

- **Reshaping for Time-Series Data**: For time-series problems, the data is often reshaped into a rolling window or a supervised learning format where the previous time steps are used to predict the next time step.

```python
import numpy as np

X = []
y = []
for i in range(len(data) - window_size):
    X.append(data[i:i + window_size])
    y.append(data[i + window_size])

X = np.array(X)
y = np.array(y)
```

- **Reshaping Image Data**: Images are typically represented as multi-dimensional arrays. If using images in deep learning, ensure the data is in the correct format (e.g., height, width, channels).

```python
from tensorflow.keras.preprocessing import image

img = image.load_img('image.jpg', target_size=(224, 224))
img_array = image.img_to_array(img)  # Convert image to array
img_array = np.expand_dims(img_array, axis=0)  # Add batch dimension
```

3. Dimensionality Reduction

Dimensionality reduction is the process of reducing the number of features (dimensions) while preserving as much information as possible. Common techniques include:

- **Principal Component Analysis (PCA)**: PCA is widely used to reduce the dimensionality of data by projecting it onto fewer principal components.

```python
from sklearn.decomposition import PCA

pca = PCA(n_components=2)
reduced_data = pca.fit_transform(data)
```

- **t-SNE**: t-SNE (t-Distributed Stochastic Neighbor Embedding) is useful for visualizing high-dimensional data in 2 or 3 dimensions.

```python
from sklearn.manifold import TSNE

tsne = TSNE(n_components=2)
tsne_data = tsne.fit_transform(data)
```

Data Visualization

Data visualization is a key step in the data handling pipeline. It allows you to explore the data, detect patterns, and gain insights, which are crucial for the data preprocessing and transformation phases.

1. Matplotlib for Basic Plots

Matplotlib is the most widely used library for creating static, animated, and interactive visualizations in Python. Some basic plots include:

- **Line Plots**: Ideal for visualizing continuous data.

```python
python

import matplotlib.pyplot as plt

plt.plot(data['column_name'])
plt.title('Line Plot')
plt.xlabel('X-axis Label')
plt.ylabel('Y-axis Label')
plt.show()
```

- **Histograms**: Great for understanding the distribution of data.

```python
python

plt.hist(data['column_name'], bins=20)
plt.title('Histogram')
plt.xlabel('Value')
plt.ylabel('Frequency')
plt.show()
```

2. Seaborn for Statistical Plots

Seaborn is built on top of Matplotlib and makes it easier to generate attractive statistical graphics. Examples include:

- **Boxplots**: Useful for detecting outliers and visualizing the spread of the data.

```python
python

import seaborn as sns

sns.boxplot(x='category', y='value', data=data)
```

```
plt.title('Boxplot Example')
plt.show()
```

- **Pair Plots**: Excellent for visualizing relationships between multiple variables.

```python
python
```

```
sns.pairplot(data)
plt.show()
```

3. Plotly for Interactive Visualizations

Plotly allows for the creation of interactive charts that can be embedded in web applications.

```python
python
```

```
import plotly.express as px

fig = px.scatter(data_frame=data, x='feature1', y='feature2',
color='category')
fig.show()
```

Efficient data handling is essential for deep learning workflows. By performing preprocessing steps like handling missing data, scaling, encoding categorical variables, and transforming the data through feature engineering and dimensionality reduction, you ensure that the data is ready for model training. Visualization techniques, from basic line plots to advanced interactive charts, help provide deeper insights into the dataset and aid in refining the preprocessing steps. As we continue, the goal is to have clean, transformed data that can be fed into deep learning models for accurate predictions and valuable insights.

Introduction to TensorFlow and Keras: Setting Up TensorFlow and Keras, Understanding Their Role in Deep Learning

In the world of deep learning, TensorFlow and Keras are two of the most widely used libraries for developing and deploying machine learning models. Both libraries are powerful, flexible, and designed to simplify the process of building neural networks. This section provides an overview of **TensorFlow** and **Keras**, highlighting their role in deep learning and how to set them up for use in your projects.

1. What is TensorFlow?

TensorFlow is an open-source library developed by Google for high-performance numerical computation and large-scale machine learning. TensorFlow is designed to be both flexible and scalable, making it suitable for a wide range of machine learning tasks, including deep learning, reinforcement learning, and natural language processing. TensorFlow is built around a system of multi-dimensional arrays called **tensors**, which is why it's named TensorFlow. These tensors allow for highly efficient computation, especially when working with deep neural networks.

Key Features of TensorFlow:

- **Scalability**: TensorFlow can scale across many machines, utilizing GPUs and TPUs (Tensor Processing Units) to accelerate computations.
- **Flexibility**: You can build complex, custom models using TensorFlow's low-level APIs, or use higher-level APIs to speed up model development.
- **TensorFlow Serving**: This allows for the deployment of machine learning models in production environments.
- **TensorFlow Lite**: Enables running models on mobile and embedded devices with optimized performance.
- **TensorFlow.js**: A JavaScript library for deploying machine learning models in the browser.

2. What is Keras?

Keras is an open-source, high-level neural networks API written in Python. It was initially developed as a user-friendly interface to various deep learning backends, including TensorFlow, Theano, and Microsoft Cognitive Toolkit (CNTK). Keras is now tightly integrated into TensorFlow and is the recommended API for building deep learning models in TensorFlow.

Key Features of Keras:

- **Simplicity**: Keras is designed to be easy to use, with clear and concise syntax that allows for rapid prototyping of neural networks.
- **Modularity**: Models in Keras are constructed using building blocks like layers, optimizers, and activation functions.
- **Extensibility**: While Keras simplifies model building, it also provides ways to extend its functionality for more complex models.
- **Pre-trained Models**: Keras includes access to a wide range of pre-trained models for image and text processing tasks, making it easier to use transfer learning for deep learning applications.

3. The Role of TensorFlow and Keras in Deep Learning

TensorFlow and Keras are pivotal in deep learning due to the following reasons:

- **TensorFlow** provides the backend infrastructure and low-level functionality to build, train, and deploy machine learning models at scale. It offers high-level abstractions for neural networks but also allows for low-level operations when more control is needed.
- **Keras**, as a high-level wrapper over TensorFlow, simplifies the process of defining and training deep learning models. It abstracts much of the complexity involved in model development, enabling users to focus on the architecture and design of the models.

In essence, **TensorFlow** is the engine that powers machine learning, while **Keras** provides a streamlined interface to build models, making the deep learning workflow faster and more accessible.

4. Setting Up TensorFlow and Keras
Step 1: **Installing TensorFlow**
To start using TensorFlow, you'll need to install it. The installation process is straightforward, especially when using Python's package manager, pip.

1. Open a terminal or command prompt.
2. Install TensorFlow using the following command:

```bash
pip install tensorflow
```

This command will install TensorFlow and Keras (since Keras is included in TensorFlow starting from version 2.0). If you need to install a specific version, you can specify it like so:

```bash
pip install tensorflow==2.11
```

Alternatively, if you're using a **GPU** for acceleration, you can install the GPU-enabled version of TensorFlow:

```bash
pip install tensorflow-gpu
```

Note: For the GPU version, ensure that your system has the necessary NVIDIA software stack (CUDA, cuDNN) installed for TensorFlow to work effectively with your GPU.

Step 2: **Verifying the Installation**

Once installed, it's important to verify that TensorFlow is correctly set up.

To verify the installation:

1. Open a Python shell or Jupyter notebook.
2. Type the following code to check TensorFlow's version and confirm that it's working:

```python
import tensorflow as tf
print("TensorFlow version:", tf.__version__)
```

You should see the version of TensorFlow printed, which confirms the successful installation.

Step 3: **Setting Up Keras**

As mentioned earlier, Keras comes bundled with TensorFlow starting from TensorFlow version 2.0. Therefore, once you have installed Tensor-Flow, you can use Keras directly via the tensorflow.keras submodule.

To verify Keras, simply import it from TensorFlow as follows:

```python
from tensorflow import keras
```

Now you can start using Keras functions to build neural networks.

5. Basic Workflow with TensorFlow and Keras

With TensorFlow and Keras installed, let's go over the basic workflow to define, compile, and train a neural network model. We'll also cover model evaluation and prediction.

Step 1: **Importing Libraries**

Before starting, make sure to import the required libraries for building and training models.

```python
python
```

```python
import tensorflow as tf
from tensorflow.keras.models import Sequential
from tensorflow.keras.layers import Dense
from tensorflow.keras.optimizers import Adam
```

Step 2: **Building a Neural Network**

You can build a neural network using Keras' Sequential API. This is the simplest way to define models, where each layer is stacked on top of the previous one.

```python
python
```

```python
model = Sequential()

# Adding layers to the model
model.add(Dense(64, input_dim=8, activation='relu'))  # Input
layer + first hidden layer
model.add(Dense(32, activation='relu'))  # Second hidden layer
model.add(Dense(1, activation='sigmoid'))  # Output layer
```

In this example, the model consists of:

- An input layer with 8 features (as indicated by input_dim=8),
- Two hidden layers with ReLU activation functions,
- A sigmoid output layer (useful for binary classification).

Step 3: **Compiling the Model**

Once the model structure is defined, it needs to be compiled. This step involves specifying the optimizer, loss function, and metrics to evaluate the model.

```python
```

```python
model.compile(optimizer=Adam(learning_rate=0.001),
loss='binary_crossentropy', metrics=['accuracy'])
```

Here:

- **Adam** is used as the optimizer, which is a popular choice for training deep learning models due to its adaptive learning rate.
- **binary_crossentropy** is the loss function used for binary classification tasks.
- **accuracy** is the metric to evaluate the model during training.

Step 4: **Training the Model**

To train the model, you use the fit function, providing the training data and labels, along with the number of epochs and batch size.

```python
```

```python
model.fit(X_train, y_train, epochs=10, batch_size=32)
```

Here, X_train is the input data and y_train is the target labels. The model will train for 10 epochs with a batch size of 32.

Step 5: **Evaluating the Model**

After training, you can evaluate the model's performance on test data using the evaluate function.

```python
```

```python
test_loss, test_acc = model.evaluate(X_test, y_test)
print(f"Test Accuracy: {test_acc}")
```

Step 6: **Making Predictions**

Once the model is trained, you can use it to make predictions on new, unseen data.

```python
predictions = model.predict(X_new_data)
```

6. Advanced Usage of TensorFlow and Keras

While the example above provides a basic introduction to TensorFlow and Keras, these libraries offer advanced features for more complex deep learning workflows:

- **Custom Layers and Models**: For custom models, Keras allows you to define layers and models manually using the functional API, which is more flexible than the Sequential API.
- **Callbacks**: Keras includes callbacks such as ModelCheckpoint, EarlyStopping, and TensorBoard for monitoring the training process and avoiding overfitting.
- **Transfer Learning**: TensorFlow and Keras make it easy to use pre-trained models (e.g., ResNet, Inception) and fine-tune them for specific tasks.

TensorFlow and Keras are indispensable tools for deep learning, providing both the low-level power of TensorFlow and the user-friendly interface of Keras. Whether you're building simple neural networks or deploying sophisticated models, these libraries simplify the process while offering flexibility and scalability. The next step is to get hands-on experience by building your own models and experimenting with the various layers, optimizers, and other features that TensorFlow and Keras provide.

Fundamentals of Neural Networks

natomy of a Neural Network: Layers, Weights, and Biases
In the realm of deep learning, **neural networks** are the foundation upon which most advanced machine learning techniques are built. Understanding the anatomy of a neural network is essential to grasp how complex tasks such as image recognition, natural language processing, and predictive analytics are performed. Neural networks, modeled after the human brain, consist of multiple interconnected layers of artificial neurons that process and learn from data.

This section delves into the components that make up a neural network: **layers**, **weights**, and **biases**. We'll examine their roles, how they interact during the training process, and how they contribute to the network's ability to learn complex patterns from data.

1. What is a Neural Network?

A neural network is a computational model that mimics the way the human brain processes information. It consists of layers of neurons that transform input data into output predictions through a series of learned parameters.

In a typical **feedforward neural network** (the most common type used in deep learning), information flows from an input layer through one or more hidden layers to an output layer. Each neuron in these layers performs a simple computation, but the collective output of the network can be extraordinarily powerful.

The three key components of a neural network are:

- **Layers**: The structural building blocks of the network.
- **Weights**: The parameters that determine the strength of connections between neurons.
- **Biases**: Parameters that allow the model to make more flexible predictions.

2. Layers in a Neural Network

A neural network is composed of three main types of layers:

- **Input Layer**
- **Hidden Layers**
- **Output Layer**

Input Layer

The **input layer** receives the raw data, which can be anything from pixel values in an image to text in a document or numbers in a table. Each neuron in the input layer corresponds to a feature in the dataset. The number of neurons in the input layer corresponds to the dimensionality of the input data.

For example:

- If the input data is an image of size 28x28 pixels (grayscale), the input layer will have 784 neurons (28x28).
- If the data consists of 10 features (e.g., age, height, weight, etc.), the input layer will have 10 neurons.

Hidden Layers

The **hidden layers** are where the majority of the computation takes place. They lie between the input and output layers and consist of neurons that are responsible for detecting patterns in the data. The more hidden layers a network has, the deeper the network is, which is why these networks are called **deep neural networks** when they contain many hidden layers.

Each neuron in a hidden layer receives inputs from the neurons in the previous layer, applies a weight to each input, sums them up, and then applies an activation function to the result. This allows the network to model complex, non-linear relationships.

Output Layer

The **output layer** produces the final prediction or classification result. The number of neurons in the output layer corresponds to the number of classes (for classification tasks) or the number of outputs (for regression tasks).

For example:

- In a binary classification task (e.g., spam vs. not spam), the output layer will have one neuron with a **sigmoid activation function** that produces a value between 0 and 1.
- In a multi-class classification task (e.g., classifying images into 10 categories), the output layer will have 10 neurons, with a **softmax activation function** that outputs a probability distribution over the 10 classes.

3. Weights in a Neural Network

Weights are the learnable parameters that connect the neurons in one layer to the neurons in the subsequent layer. Each weight represents the strength of the connection between two neurons. When training a neural network, the goal is to find the optimal values for these weights so that the network can make accurate predictions.

- Each input to a neuron is multiplied by a corresponding weight. These weighted inputs are then summed together and passed through an activation function to determine the output of the neuron.
- Weights are initialized randomly before training begins and adjusted during the training process based on the error between the predicted

output and the true output (this process is done through backpropagation and gradient descent).

How Weights Work:

- During forward propagation, each neuron in the hidden layer receives inputs, multiplies them by their respective weights, and then passes the results through an activation function.
- During training, weights are adjusted based on the gradient of the loss function with respect to each weight, using an optimization technique such as **gradient descent**.

Consider a simple example with a single neuron:

```plaintext

Output = ActivationΣ((Weight_i * Input_i))
```

Where:

- **Weight_i** represents the strength of the connection between input iii and the neuron.
- **Input_i** represents the input value to the neuron (such as pixel value or feature value).
- The sum of the weighted inputs is then passed through an **activation function**.

4. Biases in a Neural Network

A **bias** is an additional learnable parameter added to the weighted sum of inputs before applying the activation function. The bias allows the model to make predictions that are independent of the input features, essentially shifting the activation function's output.

Without biases, the output of a neuron would always be strictly dependent on the weighted sum of the inputs, which could limit the network's ability to fit certain types of data. Biases provide the flexibility for the neural network to adjust the output even when all input values are zero, improving its ability to model complex data.

How Biases Work:

- For each neuron, the weighted sum of inputs is computed as follows:
- $z = \Sigma i (\text{Weight}i \cdot \text{Input}i) + \text{Bias}\text{z} = \sum_i (\text{Weight}_i \cdot \text{Input}_i) + \text{Bias}z = i\Sigma(\text{Weight}i \cdot \text{Input}i) + \text{Bias}$
- The **bias** is added to the weighted sum to allow the model to fit the data more accurately. This helps shift the output function in the direction that minimizes the error between predicted and actual values.

The bias is adjusted in the same way as the weights during the backpropagation process. Like weights, the bias is updated iteratively to reduce the error in predictions.

5. The Activation Function

An important part of the neuron is the **activation function**, which determines the output of the neuron. It introduces non-linearity into the network, allowing the neural network to learn complex patterns in data. Without an activation function, the neural network would simply be a linear model, no matter how many layers it had.

Some common activation functions are:

- **Sigmoid**: Outputs values between 0 and 1, used for binary classification.
- $\sigma(x) = 11 + e - x\sigma(x) = \frac{1}{1 + e^{-x}}\sigma(x) = 1 + e - x1$
- **ReLU (Rectified Linear Unit)**: Outputs the input directly if it's positive; otherwise, it returns zero. It's widely used due to its simplicity and ability to mitigate the vanishing gradient problem.
- $\text{ReLU}(x) = \max\Box(0,x)\text{ReLU}(x) = \max(0, x)\text{ReLU}(x) = \max(0,x)$
- **Softmax**: Used in the output layer for multi-class classification, it normalizes the output into a probability distribution across multiple

classes.

6. The Process of Forward Propagation

In a neural network, forward propagation is the process by which input data is passed through the network to produce an output. This is done layer by layer:

- The input layer receives data and sends it to the first hidden layer.
- Each hidden layer applies weights and biases, followed by an activation function, to produce an output that is passed to the next layer.
- Finally, the output layer produces the final prediction or classification result.

The forward propagation process involves calculating the weighted sum of inputs, adding the bias, and passing the result through the activation function at each layer. This process is repeated for each layer until the output layer is reached.

7. Backpropagation and Weight Updates

Once forward propagation is completed and the model generates an output, the next step is **backpropagation**. During backpropagation, the network learns by adjusting the weights and biases to minimize the error in predictions:

- The error (difference between the predicted and true output) is propagated backward through the network.
- The gradients of the error with respect to each weight and bias are computed.
- The weights and biases are updated using an optimization algorithm (like gradient descent) to reduce the error.

Through this process, the neural network gradually improves its predictions by adjusting its parameters (weights and biases) over multiple iterations (epochs).

The anatomy of a neural network—its **layers, weights,** and **biases**—forms the core of its ability to learn from data. By understanding how these components interact during forward propagation and backpropagation, you gain insight into how neural networks are able to model complex, non-linear patterns. This fundamental understanding serves as the foundation for building and optimizing deep learning models, which can solve a wide range of real-world problems. As we continue, we will explore more advanced topics, such as training techniques and optimization strategies, to refine and enhance these networks.

Understanding Forward and Backward Propagation: Simple Explanations with Visuals

In neural networks, two key processes govern the learning and prediction cycle: **forward propagation** and **backward propagation**. These processes allow the network to make predictions and improve over time through training. Both processes are essential for the functioning of deep learning models. Understanding them is crucial to comprehend how neural networks learn from data and refine their internal parameters (weights and biases) to minimize prediction errors.

This section provides a detailed yet simple explanation of forward and backward propagation, with an emphasis on how these processes work, why they are important, and how they lead to model optimization.

1. What is Forward Propagation?

Forward propagation is the process by which input data is passed through the network to generate predictions or outputs. It involves moving data from the input layer through hidden layers to the output layer. In each layer, the inputs are weighted, summed, and passed through an activation function to produce outputs, which are then fed to the next layer.

Here's a step-by-step breakdown of how forward propagation works:

Step 1: Input Data

The input data is fed into the network through the **input layer**. These could be raw features such as pixel values of an image, word embeddings for text, or numeric values for a dataset.

For example, let's consider a neural network that takes three features as input: x1, x2, and x3.

Step 2: Weighted Sum

Each input is multiplied by a corresponding weight. The weighted inputs are then summed up. This operation is the first key step in the neuron's computation.

The weighted sum for a neuron in the hidden layer is calculated as:

$$z = w_1 x_1 + w_2 x_2 + w_3 x_3 + b$$

Where:

- x_1, x_2, x_3 are the input features,
- w_1, w_2, w_3 are the weights,
- b is the bias term, and
- z is the weighted sum.

Step 3: Activation Function

The weighted sum zzz is passed through an **activation function** to introduce non-linearity and decide the neuron's output. The activation function could be **ReLU**, **sigmoid**, or **tanh**, depending on the network design.

For example, using **ReLU** as the activation function:

$$a = \mathrm{ReLU}(z) = \max(0, z)$$

The output a is then passed to the next layer, or in the case of the output layer, this is the final prediction.

Step 4: Repeating the Process

This process of multiplying inputs by weights, summing them, adding biases, and applying an activation function is repeated across all the neurons in all layers of the network, from the input layer to the output layer.

The final result of forward propagation is the output of the neural network, which could be a classification result, a regression value, or some other form of prediction depending on the task.

2. What is Backward Propagation?

While forward propagation allows the network to make predictions, **backward propagation** is the mechanism by which the network learns from its mistakes. It involves adjusting the weights and biases to minimize the error between the predicted output and the actual output.

Backward propagation works by calculating the **gradient of the loss function** with respect to each weight and bias, and then adjusting these parameters to reduce the error. This process is commonly referred to as **gradient descent**.

Here's how backward propagation works step by step:

Step 1: Calculate the Error (Loss Function)

After forward propagation, the neural network produces a prediction. The first step in backward propagation is to calculate the **error** or **loss** by comparing the predicted output with the true output (the label or ground truth). The **loss function** quantifies this error.

For example, in a regression task, we might use **Mean Squared Error (MSE)** as the loss function:

$$\text{Loss} = \frac{1}{n} \sum_{i=1}^{n} (y_{\text{pred}} - y_{\text{true}})^2$$

Where:

- y_{pred} is the predicted value,
- y_{true} is the actual value, and
- n is the number of data points.

Step 2: Compute the Gradient of the Loss Function

The next step in backward propagation is to compute the **gradient of the loss function** with respect to each weight in the network. The gradient is a measure of how much the loss would change if the weight were adjusted. Essentially, the gradient tells us the direction in which we need to adjust the weights to minimize the loss.

The gradient of the loss function with respect to a given weight www is computed using the **chain rule of calculus**. This allows the model to update each weight in the direction that reduces the error.

Step 3: Update the Weights and Biases

Once the gradients of the weights are calculated, the next step is to adjust the weights and biases using **gradient descent** or another optimization algorithm.

Gradient descent involves updating the weights in the opposite direction of the gradient to reduce the loss. The weight update rule is as follows:

$$w = w - \eta \frac{\partial \text{Loss}}{\partial w}$$

Where:

- η is the learning rate, a hyperparameter that controls the size of the weight updates,
- $\frac{\partial \text{Loss}}{\partial w}$ is the gradient of the loss with respect to the weight.

Biases are also updated in the same way, with a similar update rule:

$$b = b - \eta \frac{\partial \text{Loss}}{\partial b}$$

The learning rate determines how big each update step should be. If the learning rate is too high, the weights may change too drastically, causing the network to overshoot the optimal solution. If the learning rate is too low, the training process may take too long or get stuck in a local minimum.

Step 4: Repeat the Process (Iterative Training)

Once the weights and biases have been updated, the process repeats. Forward propagation is performed again using the updated weights, followed by another round of backward propagation to adjust the weights further. This iterative process continues for many epochs (iterations over the entire dataset) until the network converges and the error is minimized.

3. Visualizing Forward and Backward Propagation

To help clarify the concepts of forward and backward propagation, let's consider a simple neural network with one hidden layer.

Forward Propagation (Simple Example)

Imagine a network with:

- 2 input features: $x1x\_1x1$ and $x2x\_2x2$,
- 2 neurons in the hidden layer: $h1h\_1h1$ and $h2h\_2h2$,
- 1 output neuron: $ypredy\_\{\backslash text\{pred\}\}ypred$.

The steps of forward propagation look like this:

1. **Input Layer**: The input features are passed to the hidden layer neurons.
2. **Hidden Layer**: Each hidden layer neuron calculates a weighted sum of inputs, applies an activation function, and passes the result to the output layer.
3. **Output Layer**: The output neuron calculates the final prediction using the results from the hidden layer.

A simple visual representation might look like this:

```
rust

Input Layer           Hidden Layer            Output Layer
   x1 ----------------> h1   ----------------> y_pred
   x2 ----------------> h2   ---------------->
```

Backward Propagation (Visual)

During backward propagation, the error is propagated back through the network, and the weights are updated to minimize the error.

1. **Error Calculation**: The error is computed at the output layer.
2. **Gradients Computation**: Gradients are calculated with respect to each weight in the network.
3. **Weight Update**: Each weight is updated by subtracting the gradient scaled by the learning rate.

The visual of backward propagation looks like this:

```
scss

Output Layer          Hidden Layer           Input Layer
  (Error) <--------- h1   <---------------- x1
               (Gradient)              (Gradient)
  (Error) <--------- h2   <---------------- x2
```

In this way, backward propagation works its way back from the output layer to the input layer, adjusting weights and biases in each layer to reduce the overall loss.

Forward and backward propagation are the two foundational processes in neural networks. Forward propagation allows a network to make predictions, while backward propagation enables the network to learn from its mistakes by adjusting its parameters. Through multiple iterations of these processes, neural networks gradually improve, converging towards an optimal set of weights and biases. By understanding these processes in detail, you can gain deeper insights into how neural networks function, setting the stage for building and fine-tuning powerful deep learning models. As we continue, we will explore more advanced topics such as optimization algorithms, learning rates, and advanced architectures to further enhance the performance of deep learning models.

Activation Functions: Sigmoid, ReLU, tanh, Softmax, and When to Use Each

Activation functions are the heart of neural networks, determining how the weighted sum of inputs gets transformed into an output that is passed on to the next layer. Without activation functions, a neural network would essentially be a linear regression model, no matter how many layers it has. This would limit the network's ability to capture the complexity and non-linearity of real-world data.

In this section, we'll explore the most commonly used activation functions: **Sigmoid**, **ReLU**, **tanh**, and **Softmax**. We'll explain how each function works, its characteristics, and when you should use them in different network layers.

1. Sigmoid Activation Function
Formula and Graph

The **Sigmoid function** outputs values between 0 and 1, making it useful for tasks where probabilities are required. It is especially common in binary classification problems.

The formula for the sigmoid function is:

$$\sigma(x) = \frac{1}{1 + e^{-x}}$$

Where:

- x is the input to the neuron (the weighted sum of inputs and bias).

The graph of the sigmoid function has an **S-shape** and asymptotically approaches 0 and 1 as xxx moves towards negative or positive infinity, respectively.

Characteristics of Sigmoid

- **Range**: (0, 1)
- **Non-linearity**: Yes, it introduces non-linearity into the network.
- **Derivatives**: The derivative of the sigmoid function is relatively simple and can be expressed as:

$$\sigma'(x) = \sigma(x) \cdot (1 - \sigma(x))$$

- **Saturated region**: The function has a **saturated region** around 0, where the gradients are very small (this is called the vanishing gradient problem), making it difficult for the network to learn.

When to Use Sigmoid

- **Binary classification**: It is most commonly used in the output layer for binary classification problems. Since its output lies between 0 and 1, it can be interpreted as the probability of a class, making it ideal for binary outcomes.
- **Logistic regression models**: Sigmoid is also used in logistic regression,

where it predicts the probability of a class belonging to one of two possible outcomes.

2. ReLU (Rectified Linear Unit) Activation Function
Formula and Graph

The **ReLU function** is one of the most popular activation functions in modern neural networks due to its simplicity and effectiveness. It outputs 0 for negative values and outputs the input value itself for positive values.

The formula for ReLU is:

$$\text{ReLU}(x) = \max(0, x)$$

Where:

- x is the input to the neuron.

The graph of the ReLU function is a **piecewise linear function** with a slope of 0 for negative values and a slope of 1 for positive values.

Characteristics of ReLU

- **Range**: $[0, \infty)$ — it outputs 0 for any negative input and the input value itself for any positive input.
- **Non-linearity**: Yes, it introduces non-linearity into the network.
- **Derivatives**: The derivative of ReLU is 0 for negative inputs and 1 for positive inputs.

$$\text{ReLU}'(x) = \begin{cases} 0 & \text{if } x < 0 \\ 1 & \text{if } x > 0 \end{cases}$$

- **Efficient and fast**: ReLU is computationally efficient and helps mitigate the vanishing gradient problem. Unlike sigmoid, it does not saturate for positive values.

When to Use ReLU

- **Hidden layers**: ReLU is commonly used in the hidden layers of neural networks. It is effective for most deep learning tasks and allows networks to model complex data by introducing non-linearity.
- **Deep networks**: Due to its computational efficiency and simplicity, ReLU is the go-to choice for most deep learning models, especially convolutional neural networks (CNNs) and deep feedforward networks.

3. Tanh (Hyperbolic Tangent) Activation Function
Formula and Graph

The **tanh** function is a scaled version of the sigmoid function. It outputs values between -1 and 1, making it zero-centered, which helps with faster convergence during training.

The formula for tanh is:

$$\tanh(x) = \frac{2}{1 + e^{-2x}} - 1$$

This produces outputs in the range (-1, 1), unlike the sigmoid, which outputs values between 0 and 1.

Characteristics of tanh

- Range: (-1, 1) — outputs are centered around 0.
- Non-linearity: Yes, like sigmoid, it introduces non-linearity into the network.
- Derivatives: The derivative of tanh is:

$$\tanh'(x) = 1 - \tanh^2(x)$$

When to Use tanh

- **Hidden layers**: Tanh is commonly used in the hidden layers of deep networks when the zero-centered nature of the output helps prevent bias in the learning process. It is often preferred over sigmoid because its outputs range from -1 to 1, which can lead to faster convergence during training.

- **Sequence modeling**: It has historically been used in recurrent neural networks (RNNs) due to its ability to model both positive and negative information.

4. Softmax Activation Function

Formula and Graph

The **Softmax function** is primarily used in the output layer of multi-class classification problems. It converts a vector of raw scores (also called logits) into a probability distribution, where the sum of all output values equals 1. This makes it ideal for classification tasks where each class has a probability of being the correct one.

The formula for softmax is:

$$\text{Softmax}(z_i) = \frac{e^{z_i}}{\sum_j e^{z_j}}$$

Where:

- z_i represents the raw score for class i,
- The denominator is the sum of the exponentials of all raw scores.

The output of the softmax function represents a probability distribution across multiple classes.

Characteristics of Softmax

- **Range**: [0, 1] — each output is between 0 and 1, representing the probability of the respective class.
- **Non-linearity**: Yes, it introduces non-linearity into the network.
- **Sum to 1**: The sum of all output probabilities equals 1, which is a desirable property for classification tasks.

When to Use Softmax

- **Multi-class classification**: Softmax is typically used in the output layer of neural networks for **multi-class classification problems**. It is used when the model needs to predict one of several classes (e.g., image classification, text classification).
- **Exclusive classes**: Softmax assumes that the classes are mutually exclusive, meaning the input data belongs to only one class.

5. Choosing the Right Activation Function

The selection of an activation function depends on the specific needs of the neural network and the task at hand. Here are some guidelines for choosing between them:

Sigmoid:

- Use for **binary classification** (output between 0 and 1).
- Not ideal for hidden layers due to the vanishing gradient problem.

ReLU:

- Use in the **hidden layers** of most deep neural networks, especially for tasks such as image recognition, text analysis, and speech processing.
- Fast and effective in training deep networks, but sensitive to outliers (leading to the "dying ReLU" problem).

Tanh:

- Use in hidden layers when you need **zero-centered outputs**.
- Can be more effective than sigmoid because its output range helps prevent gradients from vanishing too quickly.
- Still suffers from vanishing gradients for extreme input values.

Softmax:

- Use in the **output layer** for **multi-class classification** problems.
- Ideal for problems where each class has a probability and the model predicts one of several possible categories.

Activation functions play a crucial role in deep learning models by enabling them to learn complex patterns in data. By introducing non-linearity, they allow neural networks to approximate any function. Understanding when and where to use each activation function—whether it's sigmoid, ReLU, tanh, or softmax—depends on the task at hand, whether it's binary classification, multi-class classification, or regression. As we continue, we will explore how these activation functions interact within the layers of a network and how to address challenges like vanishing gradients to make our models even more effective.

Loss Functions: Mean Squared Error, Cross-Entropy, and Others; Choosing the Right Loss Function

Loss functions are fundamental in deep learning, serving as the measure of how well the model's predictions match the actual outcomes. During training, the model seeks to minimize the loss function through an optimization process, typically using gradient descent. The choice of loss function can significantly impact the model's performance, so it is essential to understand the different types and when to use them.

In this section, we'll explore common loss functions used in deep learning, including **Mean Squared Error (MSE)**, **Cross-Entropy**, and others. We'll also discuss how to choose the most appropriate loss function for a given task.

1. Mean Squared Error (MSE)

Formula and Explanation

The **Mean Squared Error (MSE)** loss function is commonly used in **regression problems**. It measures the average of the squared differences between the predicted values and the actual values (or targets). MSE penalizes large errors more than smaller ones due to the squaring of the differences.

The formula for MSE is:

$$\mathrm{MSE}(y, \hat{y}) = \frac{1}{n} \sum_{i=1}^{n} (y_i - \hat{y}_i)^2$$

Where:

- y_i is the actual value (ground truth),
- $\hat{y}_i$ is the predicted value,
- n is the number of data points.

Characteristics of MSE

- **Sensitivity to outliers**: Since MSE squares the differences, larger errors have a more significant impact on the loss value. This makes MSE particularly sensitive to outliers.
- **Differentiability**: MSE is differentiable everywhere, which makes it suitable for gradient-based optimization techniques like gradient descent.

When to Use MSE

- **Regression problems**: MSE is the go-to loss function for regression tasks, where the goal is to predict a continuous value. Examples include predicting house prices, stock prices, or temperature forecasting.
- **Error penalization**: It is effective when the error distribution is Gaussian, and larger errors should be penalized more heavily.

2. Cross-Entropy Loss
Formula and Explanation
Cross-Entropy Loss (also known as **log loss**) is the most widely used loss function for **classification problems**, especially when the target is

categorical. It measures the difference between the true label distribution and the predicted probability distribution. The cross-entropy loss is most commonly used in conjunction with the **Softmax activation** function in multi-class classification tasks.

For a binary classification problem, the formula for cross-entropy is:

$$\text{Binary Cross-Entropy} = -\frac{1}{n} \sum_{i=1}^{n} [y_i \log(\hat{y}_i) + (1 - y_i) \log(1 - \hat{y}_i)]$$

For multi-class classification, the formula generalizes to:

$$\text{Categorical Cross-Entropy} = -\sum_{i=1}^{n} \sum_{c=1}^{C} y_{ic} \log(\hat{y}_{ic})$$

Where:

- y_i is the true label,
- $\hat{y}_i$ is the predicted probability,
- C is the number of classes.

Characteristics of Cross-Entropy Loss

- **Probabilistic interpretation**: Cross-entropy loss is particularly suited for problems where the output represents a probability distribution. It encourages the model to output high probabilities for the correct class and low probabilities for incorrect ones.
- **Sensitivity to class imbalance**: Cross-entropy is sensitive to imbalances in the class distribution, which may require adjustments (like using weighted cross-entropy or resampling techniques).
- **Differentiability**: Like MSE, cross-entropy loss is differentiable and suitable for gradient-based optimization.

When to Use Cross-Entropy

- **Binary classification**: For binary classification tasks, cross-entropy is used with a sigmoid activation function in the output layer.

- **Multi-class classification**: In multi-class classification tasks, cross-entropy is used in combination with the softmax function to compute probabilities for each class.

- **Text classification and image classification**: Common applications include classifying emails as spam or not spam, categorizing images into different classes, and natural language processing (NLP) tasks such as sentiment analysis.

3. Hinge Loss

Formula and Explanation

The **Hinge Loss** is primarily used for **Support Vector Machines (SVMs)** but can also be applied to certain types of neural networks, especially for binary classification tasks. It is designed to penalize predictions that are on the wrong side of the decision boundary, especially for "hard margin" SVMs.

The formula for hinge loss is:

$$\text{Hinge Loss} = \sum_{i=1}^{n} \max(0, 1 - y_i \hat{y}_i)$$

Where:

- y_i is the true label ($+1$ or -1),
- $\hat{y}_i$ is the predicted label (not a probability, but rather the raw output of the decision function).

Characteristics of Hinge Loss

- **Binary classification**: Hinge loss is used for binary classification tasks with outputs that are not probabilities but rather decision values (for instance, from an SVM classifier).

- **Margin-based learning**: The hinge loss encourages the model to correctly classify points and maximize the margin between classes.

When to Use Hinge Loss

- **Support Vector Machines (SVMs):** Hinge loss is primarily used in SVMs, but it can also be applied in neural networks designed for binary classification tasks where the model outputs decision values instead of probabilities.

4. Mean Absolute Error (MAE)
Formula and Explanation

The **Mean Absolute Error (MAE)** is another loss function used in **regression tasks**. It is similar to MSE but instead of squaring the error, it takes the absolute value of the differences between the predicted and actual values. This makes it less sensitive to outliers compared to MSE.

The formula for MAE is:

$$\mathrm{MAE}(y, \hat{y}) = \frac{1}{n} \sum_{i=1}^{n} |y_i - \hat{y}_i|$$

Characteristics of MAE

- **Robust to outliers:** MAE does not penalize large errors as much as MSE, making it more robust to outliers.
- **Linear error penalization:** MAE treats all errors equally, meaning that large and small errors contribute equally to the total loss.

When to Use MAE

- **Robust regression:** MAE is ideal when the data contains outliers, and you want a loss function that is less sensitive to them.
- **Prediction accuracy over error distribution:** When the magnitude of error is more important than the nature of the error distribution,

MAE can be preferred over MSE.

5. Huber Loss

Formula and Explanation

The **Huber Loss** is a combination of MSE and MAE, designed to be more robust to outliers than MSE but still sensitive to smaller errors like MSE. It uses MSE for small errors and switches to MAE for large errors, thus offering the best of both worlds.

The formula for Huber loss is:

$$\text{Huber Loss}(y, \hat{y}) = \begin{cases} \frac{1}{2}(y_i - \hat{y}_i)^2 & \text{for } |y_i - \hat{y}_i| \leq \delta \\ \delta |y_i - \hat{y}_i| - \frac{1}{2}\delta^2 & \text{for } |y_i - \hat{y}_i| > \delta \end{cases}$$

Where δ is a threshold that determines when the loss function switches from quadratic to linear.

Characteristics of Huber Loss

- **Combination of MSE and MAE**: Huber loss behaves like MSE for small errors and like MAE for large errors, making it robust to outliers while still penalizing small errors.
- **Smoothness**: Unlike MAE, Huber loss is differentiable everywhere, making it more suitable for gradient-based optimization.

When to Use Huber Loss

- **Regression with outliers**: Huber loss is ideal when you have a regression task with outliers, and you want to balance the sensitivity to outliers and small errors.
- **Stable optimization**: It is useful when you want to ensure stable training in the presence of large errors without overly penalizing them.

6. Choosing the Right Loss Function

Choosing the right loss function is crucial for the success of your deep learning model. Here's a guide to help you choose:

- **For regression tasks**: Use **MSE** or **MAE** depending on whether you want to penalize larger errors more or have a more robust loss function to outliers.
- **For classification tasks**:
- Use **binary cross-entropy** for binary classification.
- Use **categorical cross-entropy** for multi-class classification problems.
- **For robust regression**: Use **Huber loss** to mitigate the influence of outliers while keeping stable training.
- **For SVMs and margin-based classifiers**: Use **hinge loss**.

The choice ultimately depends on the specific nature of the task, the distribution of the data, and the model's sensitivity to errors.

As we continue to build deeper understanding and techniques in deep learning, loss functions will remain a key area to explore. Adjusting them based on your model's needs can enhance performance and speed up convergence.

Gradient Descent and Optimization Techniques: Basics of Optimization, Including Batch Gradient Descent, Stochastic Gradient Descent (SGD), and Adam

Optimization is at the heart of deep learning. Once a loss function has been selected, the next task is to find the optimal parameters (weights and biases) that minimize the loss function. This is where optimization algorithms like **Gradient Descent (GD)** come into play. In deep learning, gradient descent algorithms iteratively adjust the model's parameters to reduce the loss.

In this section, we will explore the core concepts of optimization in deep learning, including various types of gradient descent methods: **Batch Gradient Descent, Stochastic Gradient Descent (SGD)**, and **Adam**. We'll also look at how these methods differ and when to use each.

1. Gradient Descent Basics
What is Gradient Descent?

Gradient descent is an iterative optimization algorithm used to minimize a loss function by adjusting the model's parameters in the direction of the steepest decrease in the loss function. This "steepest descent" is achieved by calculating the **gradient** (or derivative) of the loss function with respect to the parameters.

The basic idea behind gradient descent is to update the parameters (weights and biases) in small steps towards the minimum of the loss function. The size of these steps is controlled by the **learning rate** (α), which determines how big the steps are.

The update rule for gradient descent is:

$$\theta = \theta - \alpha \cdot \nabla_\theta J(\theta)$$

Where:

- θ are the model parameters (weights and biases),
- α is the learning rate,
- $\nabla_\theta J(\theta)$ is the gradient of the loss function $J(\theta)$ with respect to θ.

What is a Gradient?

A gradient is a vector of partial derivatives of the loss function with respect to each parameter. It tells you the slope or rate of change of the loss function, indicating which direction to move the parameters to decrease the loss. If the gradient is large in a particular direction, the loss is increasing steeply in that direction, so the model needs to update in the opposite direction to reduce the loss.

2. Batch Gradient Descent (BGD)
What is Batch Gradient Descent?

In **Batch Gradient Descent (BGD)**, the entire training dataset is used to compute the gradient of the loss function at each step. The model parameters are updated after evaluating the gradients over the entire dataset.

Formula

The update rule for BGD is:

$$\theta = \theta - \alpha \cdot \frac{1}{m} \sum_{i=1}^{m} \nabla_\theta J(\theta; x^{(i)}, y^{(i)})$$

Where:

- m is the total number of training examples,
- $x^{(i)}, y^{(i)}$ are the features and labels for the i-th training example.

Characteristics of BGD

- **Deterministic**: Since BGD uses the entire dataset to calculate the gradient, the updates are the same for each run (if the data is unchanged).
- **Slow for large datasets**: For large datasets, BGD can be very slow because it requires computing the gradient over the whole dataset before updating the parameters.
- **Convergence**: BGD guarantees convergence to the global minimum for convex loss functions, and to a local minimum for non-convex functions, which is typical in deep learning.

When to Use BGD

- **Small datasets**: BGD is effective when you have a small dataset that can be processed in memory without significant performance bottlenecks.

3. Stochastic Gradient Descent (SGD)

What is Stochastic Gradient Descent (SGD)?

Stochastic Gradient Descent (SGD) is a variation of gradient descent where the model parameters are updated using only a single training example at a time, instead of the entire dataset. This makes SGD much faster than BGD because it doesn't need to process the whole dataset before making an update.

Formula

The update rule for SGD is:

The update rule for SGD is:

$$\theta = \theta - \alpha \cdot \nabla_\theta J(\theta; x^{(i)}, y^{(i)})$$

Where $(x^{(i)}, y^{(i)})$ is a single training example.

Characteristics of SGD

- **Faster convergence**: Since SGD uses only one training example for each update, the model updates much more frequently and often reaches a solution faster than BGD.
- **Noisy updates**: The updates are more "noisy" due to the random selection of training examples. This randomness can help escape local minima and potentially find a better solution, but it can also make the training process less stable.
- **Frequent updates**: In contrast to BGD, which only updates after processing the entire dataset, SGD updates after every training example, allowing for more frequent and rapid parameter adjustments.

When to Use SGD

- **Large datasets**: SGD is ideal for large datasets that cannot fit into memory because it only requires a single training example to update the model parameters.
- **Online learning**: SGD is suitable for online learning scenarios, where data is available in a stream, and the model updates continuously.

4. Mini-Batch Gradient Descent

What is Mini-Batch Gradient Descent?

Mini-Batch Gradient Descent is a compromise between **Batch Gradient Descent** and **Stochastic Gradient Descent**. Instead of using the entire dataset (as in BGD) or a single data point (as in SGD), mini-batch gradient descent uses a small random subset of the training data, known as a **mini-batch**, to compute the gradient and update the model parameters.

Formula

The update rule for mini-batch gradient descent is:

$$\theta = \theta - \alpha \cdot \frac{1}{m} \sum_{i=1}^{m} \nabla_\theta J(\theta; x^{(i)}, y^{(i)})$$

Where:

- m is the size of the mini-batch (a small batch of training samples),
- $x^{(i)}, y^{(i)}$ are the features and labels for the i-th training example.

Characteristics of Mini-Batch Gradient Descent

- **Efficient computation**: Mini-batch gradient descent strikes a balance between computational efficiency and model performance, making it one of the most commonly used optimization techniques in deep learning.
- **More stable than SGD**: The updates in mini-batch gradient descent are less noisy than those in pure SGD, leading to more stable training while maintaining the fast convergence of SGD.
- **Parallelization**: Mini-batches allow for parallel computation across multiple processors or GPUs, further speeding up the training process.

When to Use Mini-Batch Gradient Descent

- **Large datasets**: Mini-batch gradient descent is ideal for large datasets, especially when using GPUs to speed up computation.

- **Standard in deep learning**: It is widely used in deep learning frameworks because it offers a good trade-off between convergence speed and computational efficiency.

5. Adam Optimizer (Adaptive Moment Estimation)

What is Adam?

The **Adam (Adaptive Moment Estimation)** optimizer combines the best features of two other optimizers: **Adagrad** and **RMSprop**. It computes adaptive learning rates for each parameter by keeping track of both the first moment (the mean) and the second moment (the uncentered variance) of the gradients.

Formula

The update rule for Adam is:

$$\hat{m}_t = \beta_1 \hat{m}_{t-1} + (1 - \beta_1)g_t$$

$$\hat{v}_t = \beta_2 \hat{v}_{t-1} + (1 - \beta_2)g_t^2$$

$$\theta = \theta - \alpha \frac{\hat{m}_t}{\sqrt{\hat{v}_t} + \epsilon}$$

Where:

- g_t is the gradient at time step t,
- $\hat{m}_t$ and $\hat{v}_t$ are the estimates of the first and second moments,
- α is the learning rate,
- β_1 and β_2 are hyperparameters controlling the exponential decay rates of the moment estimates,
- ϵ is a small constant to prevent division by zero.

Characteristics of Adam

- **Adaptive learning rates**: Adam adjusts the learning rate for each parameter based on the first and second moments of the gradients, making it more efficient in terms of both speed and memory usage.
- **Fast convergence**: It typically converges faster than traditional gradi-

ent descent methods, especially for complex deep learning models.

- **Less manual tuning**: Adam usually requires fewer adjustments to the learning rate and works well with default parameter values in most cases.

When to Use Adam

- **General deep learning tasks**: Adam is often the default optimizer used in deep learning frameworks for a variety of tasks, especially for large-scale and complex models.
- **When training deep neural networks**: Adam performs well in tasks like image classification, language modeling, and other large-scale applications where large datasets and complex architectures are involved.

6. Choosing the Right Optimization Technique

Each optimization technique has its strengths and is best suited for specific types of problems. Here's a quick summary of when to use each:

- **Batch Gradient Descent**: Use for small datasets and when computational resources allow for full dataset processing at each step.
- **Stochastic Gradient Descent (SGD)**: Use for very large datasets, real-time data, or when the model needs to converge quickly.
- **Mini-Batch Gradient Descent**: This is typically the most common choice for deep learning, balancing speed, stability, and memory efficiency.
- **Adam**: Best for deep learning with large, complex datasets and models, often the go-to for most practitioners.

By understanding these optimization techniques, you can select the best method suited to your deep learning task, ensuring faster convergence and better model performance.

As we continue with advanced techniques in the following chapters, optimization will remain a central concept, and fine-tuning your model's learning process is key to achieving optimal results.

Building Your First Deep Learning Model

Constructing Models with Keras: Model Creation, Compiling, and Training

In this chapter, we will walk through the essential steps of constructing a deep learning model using **Keras**, one of the most popular deep learning libraries. Keras provides a high-level interface for building and training neural networks, and it is highly flexible and easy to use for both beginners and experts in deep learning. Keras is built on top of **TensorFlow**, which allows it to leverage the powerful computational capabilities of TensorFlow while maintaining a user-friendly interface.

Building a deep learning model is a structured process that involves the following steps:

1. **Model Creation**: Defining the structure of the neural network.
2. **Compiling the Model**: Configuring the model with loss functions, optimizers, and evaluation metrics.
3. **Training the Model**: Feeding the data into the model and adjusting the weights to minimize the loss.

By the end of this chapter, you will have a clear understanding of how to use Keras to build and train a deep learning model from scratch.

1. Model Creation in Keras

The first step in building any neural network is to define the architecture of the model. The architecture consists of layers, and each layer has specific functions such as neurons, activation functions, and weights. In Keras, you can define models using either the **Sequential API** or the **Functional API**.

Using the Sequential API

The **Sequential model** is a linear stack of layers, where each layer has exactly one input tensor and one output tensor. It's a simple way to define a model when the architecture is a plain stack of layers, which is often the case for many standard deep learning problems such as image classification.

The basic syntax to create a model using Keras' Sequential API is:

```python
from keras.models import Sequential
from keras.layers import Dense, Flatten

# Create the Sequential model
model = Sequential()

# Add layers to the model
model.add(Flatten(input_shape=(28, 28)))  # Flatten the input
into a vector
model.add(Dense(128, activation='relu'))  # Fully connected
hidden layer with ReLU activation
model.add(Dense(10, activation='softmax'))  # Output layer with
softmax activation (for classification)
```

- **Flatten Layer**: This layer is used to flatten the 2D input (e.g., images) into a 1D vector to pass to the fully connected layers.
- **Dense Layer**: This is a fully connected layer. It has a specified number of neurons (e.g., 128) and an activation function, in this case, **ReLU** (Rectified Linear Unit).
- **Activation Function**: The activation function determines the output of a neuron. Common activations include **ReLU, sigmoid, softmax,** etc. ReLU is typically used in hidden layers, and softmax is used in the output layer for multi-class classification.

Using the Functional API

The **Functional API** is more flexible than the Sequential API and allows you to build more complex models where layers can have multiple inputs or outputs. Here's an example of creating a model with the Functional API:

```python
from keras.models import Model
from keras.layers import Input, Dense

# Define the input layer
inputs = Input(shape=(28, 28))

# Add layers
x = Flatten()(inputs)   # Flatten the input
x = Dense(128, activation='relu')(x)   # Fully connected layer
outputs = Dense(10, activation='softmax')(x)   # Output layer

# Create the model
model = Model(inputs=inputs, outputs=outputs)
```

With the Functional API, you have more control over the architecture, making it suitable for more complex models, such as those with multiple branches or skip connections.

2. Compiling the Model

After defining the architecture of the model, the next step is to **compile** the model. Compiling the model involves specifying:

1. **Optimizer**: The algorithm used to minimize the loss function (e.g., SGD, Adam, RMSprop).
2. **Loss Function**: The function that measures how well the model's predictions match the target values. It should align with the type of problem you are solving (e.g., mean squared error for regression, cross-entropy for classification).
3. **Metrics**: The metrics you want to track during training, such as

accuracy or precision.

Here's an example of compiling a Keras model:

```python
python
```

```python
model.compile(optimizer='adam',
              loss='sparse_categorical_crossentropy',
              metrics=['accuracy'])
```

- **Optimizer**: adam is one of the most widely used optimizers in deep learning because it adapts the learning rate based on the gradient. Adam is generally a good default choice.
- **Loss Function**: sparse_categorical_crossentropy is used for multi-class classification problems where the target labels are integers. If you have one-hot encoded labels, you would use categorical_crossentropy instead.
- **Metrics**: accuracy is a commonly used metric for classification tasks to track how many predictions were correct.

Keras offers a wide variety of loss functions and optimizers, and selecting the right combination depends on the problem you are solving.

3. Training the Model

Once the model is compiled, the next step is to **train** it using the training data. In this phase, the model learns the weights that minimize the loss function by adjusting its parameters through backpropagation and gradient descent.

The basic syntax for training a Keras model is:

```python
python
```

```
model.fit(x_train, y_train, epochs=10, batch_size=32,
validation_data=(x_val, y_val))
```

- **x_train**: The input features for training (e.g., images).
- **y_train**: The target labels for training (e.g., class labels).
- **epochs**: The number of times the entire dataset is passed through the model. Increasing the number of epochs can lead to better learning, but it may also cause overfitting.
- **batch_size**: The number of samples per gradient update. Smaller batch sizes allow the model to update more frequently, while larger batch sizes are more computationally efficient.
- **validation_data**: A tuple of data used to evaluate the model's performance during training. This helps track how well the model generalizes to unseen data.

During training, Keras provides real-time feedback, including the loss and accuracy for each epoch, which helps you monitor the progress of model optimization.

4. Evaluating the Model

After training the model, it's important to evaluate its performance on a separate test dataset to determine how well it generalizes to new, unseen data. You can use the evaluate method in Keras to do this:

```python
test_loss, test_acc = model.evaluate(x_test, y_test)
print('Test Loss:', test_loss)
print('Test Accuracy:', test_acc)
```

- **x_test** and **y_test** are the features and labels of the test set.
- The model will return two values: the **test loss** and **test accuracy**.

These metrics give you an understanding of how well the model has learned from the data.

5. Making Predictions

Once the model has been trained and evaluated, you can use it to make predictions on new data. This is done using the predict method:

python

```
predictions = model.predict(x_new)
```

- **x_new** is the input data for which you want to make predictions (e.g., new images).
- The output, **predictions**, will contain the predicted probabilities for each class, and you can apply a threshold or take the argmax (for classification tasks) to determine the final class.

6. Model Saving and Loading

It's essential to save your trained model for future use. You can save the model in Keras using the save method:

python

```
model.save('my_model.h5')
```

This saves the model architecture, weights, and training configuration to a file. To load a saved model, use the load_model function:

python

```
from keras.models import load_model
model = load_model('my_model.h5')
```

This makes it easy to deploy your trained model to production or continue training at a later point.

By following these steps, you've learned how to build a deep learning model using Keras, from defining the model architecture to compiling, training, and evaluating it. Keras abstracts away much of the complexity involved in building neural networks, allowing you to focus on designing and experimenting with models rather than dealing with low-level implementation details.

In the next chapters, we will explore more advanced deep learning concepts, such as convolutional neural networks (CNNs) and recurrent neural networks (RNNs), and how to use Keras to implement these models for a variety of applications.

Evaluating Model Performance: Accuracy, Loss, Confusion Matrix, Precision, Recall

Once you have trained a deep learning model, it is crucial to evaluate its performance to understand how well it generalizes to unseen data. Evaluation metrics provide insight into the model's accuracy and effectiveness in performing the task at hand. In this section, we will cover key evaluation metrics such as **accuracy**, **loss**, **confusion matrix**, **precision**, and **recall**, and explain how to interpret them.

1. Accuracy and Loss
Accuracy
Accuracy is one of the most common and intuitive metrics used for evaluating classification models. It represents the percentage of correct predictions made by the model out of all predictions. It is calculated as:

$$\text{Accuracy} = \frac{\text{Number of Correct Predictions}}{\text{Total Number of Predictions}}$$

In Keras, accuracy is tracked automatically during training when specified as a metric. After training the model, you can evaluate the accuracy on a test dataset:

```python
test_loss, test_acc = model.evaluate(x_test, y_test)
print('Test Accuracy:', test_acc)
```

When to Use: Accuracy is useful when the dataset is balanced (i.e., all classes have roughly the same number of samples). However, for imbalanced datasets, accuracy might not reflect the true performance of the model.

Loss

Loss is a measure of how well the model's predictions match the actual values. During training, the model aims to minimize the loss function, which can be selected based on the type of problem. For classification tasks, common loss functions include **categorical cross-entropy** or **sparse categorical cross-entropy**, and for regression, **mean squared error** is often used.

```python
test_loss, test_acc = model.evaluate(x_test, y_test)
print('Test Loss:', test_loss)
```

When to Use: Loss gives an idea of how well the model is learning and whether the optimization process is effective. A lower loss indicates a better fit, but loss should be interpreted alongside other metrics such as accuracy.

2. Confusion Matrix

A **confusion matrix** provides a detailed breakdown of a classification model's performance by showing the counts of true positives, true negatives, false positives, and false negatives. It allows you to visualize the types of errors the model is making, which is critical for understanding performance in multi-class classification problems.

A confusion matrix for a binary classification problem typically looks like this:

	Predicted Positive	Predicted Negative
Actual Positive	True Positive (TP)	False Negative (FN)
Actual Negative	False Positive (FP)	True Negative (TN)

For multi-class classification, the matrix extends to a square grid, where each cell represents the count of samples from the actual class to the predicted class.

To generate a confusion matrix in Python, you can use **scikit-learn**:

```python
python

from sklearn.metrics import confusion_matrix
import seaborn as sns
import matplotlib.pyplot as plt

y_pred = model.predict(x_test)  # Model predictions
y_pred = np.argmax(y_pred, axis=1)  # Convert probabilities to
class labels
cm = confusion_matrix(y_test, y_pred)

# Plot the confusion matrix
sns.heatmap(cm, annot=True, fmt="d", cmap="Blues")
plt.xlabel('Predicted Labels')
plt.ylabel('True Labels')
plt.show()
```

When to Use: The confusion matrix is especially useful for imbalanced datasets because it shows how many false positives and false negatives are being made. It is crucial for understanding where your model is failing, particularly in multi-class problems.

3. Precision and Recall

While accuracy gives an overall measure of how often the model is correct, **precision** and **recall** provide more granular insights into model performance, especially for imbalanced datasets.

Precision

Precision measures the proportion of true positive predictions among all positive predictions made by the model. It answers the question: *Of all the positive predictions the model made, how many were actually correct?*

$$\text{Precision} = \frac{\text{True Positives}}{\text{True Positives} + \text{False Positives}}$$

Precision is important when the cost of false positives is high. For example, in email spam detection, you want to minimize the number of legitimate emails marked as spam.

Recall

Recall, also known as **sensitivity** or **true positive rate**, measures the proportion of actual positive instances that the model successfully identified. It answers the question: *Of all the actual positives, how many did the model correctly identify?*

$$\text{Recall} = \frac{\text{True Positives}}{\text{True Positives} + \text{False Negatives}}$$

Recall is crucial when the cost of false negatives is high. For example, in medical diagnoses, you want to ensure that all positive cases are identified, even if some negative cases are misclassified.

Precision-Recall Trade-off

Precision and recall often have an inverse relationship. As you increase recall by identifying more positives, you may also increase the number of false positives, thereby reducing precision. Conversely, if you increase precision by being more cautious in labeling positives, you may miss some true positives, thus lowering recall.

This trade-off is often visualized using a **Precision-Recall Curve**, which plots precision against recall for different threshold values.

In Keras, precision and recall can be tracked using the **metrics** argument when compiling the model:

```python
from keras.metrics import Precision, Recall

model.compile(optimizer='adam',
              loss='sparse_categorical_crossentropy',
              metrics=[Precision(), Recall()])
```

4. F1-Score

The **F1-score** is the harmonic mean of precision and recall. It is a single metric that combines both precision and recall into a single value, which is useful when you need to balance the two metrics.

$$\text{F1-score} = 2 \times \frac{\text{Precision} \times \text{Recall}}{\text{Precision} + \text{Recall}}$$

The F1-score is particularly useful in situations where you need a balance between precision and recall, and it is often used in tasks like information retrieval, medical testing, and anomaly detection.

```python
from sklearn.metrics import f1_score

f1 = f1_score(y_test, y_pred, average='weighted')
print('F1-score:', f1)
```

5. Receiver Operating Characteristic (ROC) Curve and AUC

For binary classification, another useful evaluation tool is the **ROC curve** (Receiver Operating Characteristic curve). It plots the **True Positive Rate (Recall)** against the **False Positive Rate (1 - Specificity)** for various thresholds. The area under the ROC curve (AUC) quantifies the overall ability of the model to discriminate between positive and negative classes.

- **AUC (Area Under the Curve)**: AUC is a measure of the model's ability to rank predictions. An AUC value of 1 means perfect predictions, while an AUC of 0.5 indicates random guessing.

To plot the ROC curve and compute AUC, you can use **scikit-learn**:

```python
from sklearn.metrics import roc_curve, auc

fpr, tpr, thresholds = roc_curve(y_test, y_pred)
roc_auc = auc(fpr, tpr)

# Plot ROC curve
plt.plot(fpr, tpr, color='darkorange', lw=2, label='ROC curve
(AUC = %0.2f)' % roc_auc)
plt.plot([0, 1], [0, 1], color='navy', lw=2, linestyle='--')
plt.xlabel('False Positive Rate')
plt.ylabel('True Positive Rate')
plt.title('Receiver Operating Characteristic (ROC) Curve')
```

```
plt.legend(loc="lower right")
plt.show()
```

Evaluating your deep learning model's performance is crucial for under-standing its effectiveness and ensuring it meets your objectives. **Accuracy** provides a quick overview, but **precision**, **recall**, and the **confusion matrix** offer deeper insights into where the model is succeeding and where it is making mistakes. The **F1-score** balances precision and recall, while the **ROC curve** and **AUC** provide additional tools for assessing the trade-off between sensitivity and specificity.

By using these metrics and understanding their implications, you can make informed decisions on how to improve your model, fine-tune its parameters, and assess its suitability for deployment in real-world applications.

Hands-On: Building a Simple Classifier

In this section, we'll walk you through the process of building a simple deep learning model for classification using Keras and TensorFlow. This hands-on example will give you practical experience with building, com-piling, training, and evaluating a neural network model for a classification task. We'll use a popular dataset called **MNIST**, which contains images of handwritten digits (0-9). By the end of this tutorial, you'll have a fully trained model that can classify images of digits.

Step 1: Importing Required Libraries

To get started, we need to import the necessary libraries. Make sure you have already set up your Python environment with TensorFlow, Keras, and other required packages.

```python
python

import numpy as np
import tensorflow as tf
from tensorflow.keras import layers, models
import matplotlib.pyplot as plt
```

In this step, we import TensorFlow, Keras (for building models), numpy for numerical operations, and matplotlib for visualizing the results.

Step 2: Loading the MNIST Dataset

The MNIST dataset is conveniently available within TensorFlow/Keras. It consists of 60,000 training images and 10,000 testing images of handwritten digits.

```python
python

# Load MNIST dataset
(x_train, y_train), (x_test, y_test) =
tf.keras.datasets.mnist.load_data()

# Normalize the pixel values to the range [0, 1]
x_train, x_test = x_train / 255.0, x_test / 255.0
```

We load the dataset, which is split into training and testing sets. Each image is a 28x28 pixel array, and the target labels are the corresponding digits (0-9). Normalization is essential to scale the pixel values between 0 and 1 for better model performance.

Step 3: Visualizing the Data

Before building the model, it's good practice to take a look at a few sample images from the dataset. This gives us an understanding of the data we're working with.

```python
python

# Plot the first 5 images in the training set
fig, ax = plt.subplots(1, 5, figsize=(12, 5))
for i in range(5):
    ax[i].imshow(x_train[i], cmap='gray')
    ax[i].set_title(f"Label: {y_train[i]}")
    ax[i].axis('off')
plt.show()
```

This code will display the first five images in the training set with their corresponding labels. This visualization helps you understand the kind of data you're working with before passing it through the neural network.

Step 4: Defining the Neural Network Architecture

Now that we have the data ready, it's time to build our model. We will create a simple feed-forward neural network (fully connected layers) with three layers:

- **Input layer**: The input layer corresponds to the flattened 28x28 images, which are turned into a 784-dimensional vector.
- **Hidden layer**: A fully connected layer with 128 neurons and ReLU activation.
- **Output layer**: A softmax layer with 10 neurons, corresponding to the 10 possible digit classes (0-9).

```python
python

# Define the model
model = models.Sequential([
    layers.Flatten(input_shape=(28, 28)),        # Flatten the
    image to a 1D vector
    layers.Dense(128, activation='relu'),        # Fully
```

```
    connected hidden layer
    layers.Dense(10, activation='softmax')         # Output layer
    with 10 classes (digits 0-9)
])
```

Here, the Flatten layer converts the 28x28 image into a 1D array, which can then be processed by the fully connected (Dense) layers. The ReLU activation function helps introduce non-linearity, and the output layer uses softmax to provide a probability distribution across the 10 possible classes.

Step 5: Compiling the Model

Once the model architecture is defined, we need to compile the model. Compilation involves setting the optimizer, the loss function, and the evaluation metrics. For classification tasks like this, we typically use **categorical cross-entropy** as the loss function and **accuracy** as the evaluation metric.

```python
# Compile the model
model.compile(optimizer='adam',
              loss='sparse_categorical_crossentropy',
              metrics=['accuracy'])
```

- **Optimizer**: We use Adam, a popular optimization algorithm that adjusts the learning rate dynamically.
- **Loss function**: We use sparse categorical cross-entropy, which is suitable for multi-class classification problems where the target is a single integer (not one-hot encoded).
- **Metrics**: We track the accuracy of the model during training and evaluation.

Step 6: Training the Model

Now that the model is compiled, we can train it using the training data. We'll use the fit function, specifying the number of epochs (iterations over the entire training dataset) and the batch size (how many samples are processed before the model's weights are updated).

python

```python
# Train the model
history = model.fit(x_train, y_train, epochs=5, batch_size=32,
validation_data=(x_test, y_test))
```

- **Epochs**: We specify that the model will be trained for 5 epochs. This means the entire training dataset will be used to update the model 5 times.
- **Batch size**: We set the batch size to 32, meaning the model will process 32 samples at a time before updating its weights.
- **Validation data**: We pass the test data to validate the model's performance during training.

Step 7: Evaluating the Model

After training the model, we evaluate its performance on the test set using the evaluate method. This will give us the loss and accuracy of the model on unseen data.

python

```python
# Evaluate the model on the test set
test_loss, test_acc = model.evaluate(x_test, y_test)
print(f"Test accuracy: {test_acc}")
```

The test_loss gives us the model's performance in terms of the loss function, and test_acc shows the accuracy on the test dataset.

Step 8: Making Predictions

Now that we have a trained model, we can use it to make predictions on new data. Here, we will make predictions on a few test images and visualize the results.

python

```
# Predict the first 5 test samples
y_pred = model.predict(x_test[:5])

# Display the results
for i in range(5):
    plt.imshow(x_test[i], cmap='gray')
    plt.title(f"Predicted: {np.argmax(y_pred[i])}, Actual:
    {y_test[i]}")
    plt.axis('off')
    plt.show()
```

The predict function returns probabilities for each class. We use np.argmax to select the class with the highest probability as the model's predicted label.

Step 9: Visualizing Training History

It is important to visualize the training history to understand how well the model is learning. We can plot the loss and accuracy curves to see if the model is improving over time or if it has overfitted.

python

```
# Plot training and validation accuracy
plt.plot(history.history['accuracy'], label='Train Accuracy')
plt.plot(history.history['val_accuracy'], label='Validation
Accuracy')
plt.title('Model Accuracy')
plt.xlabel('Epochs')
plt.ylabel('Accuracy')
plt.legend()
plt.show()
```

```
# Plot training and validation loss
plt.plot(history.history['loss'], label='Train Loss')
plt.plot(history.history['val_loss'], label='Validation Loss')
plt.title('Model Loss')
plt.xlabel('Epochs')
plt.ylabel('Loss')
plt.legend()
plt.show()
```

This will plot the training and validation accuracy and loss curves, which can help identify if the model is underfitting or overfitting.

Congratulations! You've just built a simple deep learning classifier using Keras and TensorFlow. Through this hands-on example, you've learned how to load data, define a neural network, compile and train the model, and evaluate its performance. This foundation will serve as the basis for building more complex models and tackling real-world machine learning tasks.

Remember, while this model is a simple starting point, the core principles remain the same when dealing with larger datasets or more complex models. As you move forward, you can experiment with different architectures, optimization techniques, and hyperparameters to improve the model's performance.

Saving and Loading Models: Model Serialization for Reuse

Once you've built and trained a deep learning model, it's crucial to save it so that you can reuse it later without having to retrain it from scratch. This process is called **model serialization**. In Keras and TensorFlow, saving and loading models is straightforward and highly useful, especially when dealing with large models or when you want to share or deploy the model in production environments.

In this section, we'll walk through how to save and load Keras models, ensuring that you can preserve the trained weights, architecture, and optimizer state.

Why Save and Load Models?

Saving models allows you to:

- **Reuse models**: Load the model later to make predictions on new data without needing to retrain it.
- **Share models**: Share pre-trained models with others for inference or further fine-tuning.
- **Deploy models**: Save models in a format ready for deployment in a web application or production environment.
- **Optimize for performance**: By saving models, you can save time and computational resources, especially when working with large datasets or complex models.

Step 1: Saving the Model

Keras provides the save() function to serialize a model. This function saves the entire model, including the architecture, weights, and optimizer state, which allows you to resume training from the exact point you left off.

You can save the model in two common formats: **HDF5** or **TensorFlow's SavedModel** format.

Option 1: Save as HDF5 Format

HDF5 is a popular format for storing models, especially when you want to save and load the entire model (architecture, weights, optimizer state) in a single file.

```python
# Save the model in HDF5 format
model.save('digit_classifier.h5')
```

This will create a file named digit_classifier.h5 in your current directory.

You can load it later to make predictions or resume training.

Option 2: Save as TensorFlow SavedModel Format

TensorFlow's **SavedModel** format is the default and is more robust for serving models in production. It includes not only the model weights but also metadata, which is essential for deployment.

```python
# Save the model in SavedModel format
model.save('saved_model/digit_classifier')
```

This will save the model in the directory saved_model/digit_classifier . TensorFlow will create a directory structure containing the model's architecture, weights, and other associated information.

Step 2: Loading the Model

Once a model is saved, you can load it from disk at any time, which allows you to reuse the model without retraining. Keras provides a simple function called load_model() to load a saved model.

Option 1: Load from HDF5 Format

If you saved the model in HDF5 format, you can load it as follows:

```python
from tensorflow.keras.models import load_model

# Load the saved model from HDF5 file
loaded_model = load_model('digit_classifier.h5')
```

This will load the model with its architecture, weights, and optimizer state. You can now use loaded_model just like the original model.

Option 2: Load from TensorFlow SavedModel Format

If you saved the model using TensorFlow's SavedModel format, you can load it with the following code:

```python
python
```

```python
# Load the saved model from SavedModel format
loaded_model = load_model('saved_model/digit_classifier')
```

TensorFlow automatically detects the SavedModel format and loads the model accordingly.

Step 3: Making Predictions with the Loaded Model

Once the model is loaded, you can use it to make predictions just like you did with the original model. Let's predict on a few images from the test dataset to ensure that the loaded model works as expected.

```python
python
```

```python
# Predict using the loaded model
y_pred = loaded_model.predict(x_test[:5])

# Display the predictions
for i in range(5):
    plt.imshow(x_test[i], cmap='gray')
    plt.title(f"Predicted: {np.argmax(y_pred[i])}, Actual:
    {y_test[i]}")
    plt.axis('off')
    plt.show()
```

This code will make predictions on the first five images of the test set, displaying the predicted and actual labels.

Step 4: Continuing Training with the Loaded Model

One of the great benefits of saving and loading models is the ability to continue training from the point you left off. After loading the model, you can resume training by calling the fit() method, just like before.

```python
python
```

```python
# Continue training the loaded model
loaded_model.fit(x_train, y_train, epochs=5, batch_size=32,
validation_data=(x_test, y_test))
```

This allows you to continue training the model without starting from scratch, which is especially helpful if you have a long training process or if you want to fine-tune the model further with new data.

Step 5: Saving and Loading Only Weights

In some cases, you may want to save just the **weights** of the model rather than the entire model. This is useful when you want to share or reuse only the trained weights (for example, fine-tuning a model on a new dataset).

To save just the weights, you can use the save_weights() method:

```python
python
```

```python
# Save only the model weights
model.save_weights('model_weights.h5')
```

To load the weights back into a model, you first need to define the model architecture (with the same layers and configurations) and then load the weights:

```python
python
```

```python
# Load model weights
model.load_weights('model_weights.h5')
```

This way, you can save and load only the weights while keeping the same architecture, which is often used in transfer learning or fine-tuning.

Step 6: Model Versioning and Deployment

For production deployment, it's often necessary to version your models and ensure that the correct version is being used for inference. TensorFlow's SavedModel format makes it easy to manage model versions. You can save multiple versions of the model in the same directory, and TensorFlow will keep track of them.

```python
# Save multiple versions of the model (e.g., v1, v2, etc.)
model.save('saved_model/digit_classifier_v2')
```

In deployment environments, you can load the model from a specific version, ensuring consistency between training and production.

In this section, we covered the essential techniques for saving and loading deep learning models. This practice is vital for preserving models, sharing them with others, and deploying them in production environments. Whether you're saving the entire model (architecture + weights + optimizer state) or just the model weights, understanding how to serialize models ensures that you can efficiently work with and reuse your trained models in a wide variety of scenarios.

As you continue your deep learning journey, consider saving your models frequently, especially after training for significant amounts of time, so that you don't lose progress.

Convolutional Neural Networks (CNNs) for Image Processing

I ntroduction to Convolutional Neural Networks (CNNs): How CNNs Work and Why They Are Used for Image Data

Convolutional Neural Networks (CNNs) have revolutionized the field of deep learning, particularly in the domain of image processing. They are a specialized class of neural networks designed to process data that comes in the form of multiple arrays, such as images. The design of CNNs, inspired by the visual processing mechanisms in the human brain, enables them to automatically learn hierarchical features of data, making them particularly effective for tasks like image classification, object detection, and more.

In this chapter, we will delve into the core mechanics of CNNs, explore their components, and understand why they are uniquely suited for processing images. By the end of this chapter, you will have a solid understanding of CNNs, how they differ from traditional feedforward networks, and why they are so powerful for tasks involving visual data.

What are Convolutional Neural Networks (CNNs)?

CNNs are a type of deep learning model that is particularly well-suited for image analysis tasks. They are designed to automatically and adaptively learn spatial hierarchies of features in an image through the use of convolutional layers, pooling layers, and fully connected layers. The network learns to recognize patterns, shapes, and textures at various levels of abstraction, from simple edges to complex objects.

Unlike traditional neural networks that expect data to be in a flat, one-dimensional vector, CNNs take advantage of the two-dimensional structure of images, maintaining the spatial relationships between pixels. This allows CNNs to preserve and exploit the spatial hierarchy present in image data, which is critical for tasks such as facial recognition, object detection, and image segmentation.

How Do Convolutional Neural Networks Work?

CNNs work by using multiple layers, each with specific functions that allow the network to learn progressively more complex representations of the input image. The primary building blocks of CNNs include:

1. Convolutional Layer

The convolutional layer is the cornerstone of CNNs. It uses a mathematical operation called **convolution**, which involves sliding a small filter (or kernel) across the input image to extract local features. These filters are learned during the training process and are used to detect various features, such as edges, corners, textures, and patterns.

Each filter is a small matrix (e.g., 3x3, 5x5) that performs element-wise multiplication with the image (or the feature map from the previous layer) to generate a new set of feature maps. The convolutional operation helps CNNs preserve the spatial structure of the input, making them ideal for processing images.

Example of Convolution

Suppose we have a 5x5 input image matrix and a 3x3 filter. The convolution operation involves sliding the filter across the input image, performing element-wise multiplication at each position, and summing the results. This results in a 3x3 feature map that represents certain local features of the image.

2. Activation Function

After the convolution operation, the result is passed through an activation function, typically the **ReLU (Rectified Linear Unit)** function. The ReLU activation introduces non-linearity into the network, allowing it to learn more complex patterns. It works by setting all negative values in the feature map to zero, effectively allowing only positive values to pass through.

3. Pooling Layer

The pooling layer is used to reduce the spatial dimensions of the feature maps (i.e., downsampling), which helps reduce computational cost, control overfitting, and provide an abstraction of features. The most common type of pooling is **max pooling**, which selects the maximum value from a defined window (usually 2x2) as the representative value for that region.

For example, if you apply a 2x2 max pooling operation to a 4x4 feature map, you will get a 2x2 downsampled feature map. Pooling helps CNNs become invariant to small translations in the image, making the model more robust.

4. Fully Connected Layer

After a series of convolutional and pooling layers, the final feature maps are typically flattened into a one-dimensional vector and passed through one or more fully connected layers. These layers perform the final decision-making for the model. The fully connected layer connects every neuron in the previous layer to every neuron in the current layer, allowing the network to combine the extracted features into a final prediction.

For example, in an image classification task, the fully connected layers will use the features extracted by the convolutional layers to classify the image into one of several categories (e.g., "cat," "dog," "car").

Why Are CNNs Used for Image Data?

CNNs are specifically designed to take advantage of the structure of image data, making them particularly effective for image processing tasks. Here are the key reasons why CNNs are so well-suited for working with images:

1. Local Receptive Fields

Convolutional layers in a CNN use **local receptive fields**, meaning each neuron in the layer only looks at a small region of the input image (a local patch). This is highly beneficial for image data, where local features (such as edges, textures, and corners) are crucial for understanding the content of the image. Local receptive fields allow CNNs to focus on different parts of the image without needing to process every pixel in the entire image at once.

2. Weight Sharing

CNNs use **weight sharing**, which means that the same filter is applied to different parts of the image. This significantly reduces the number of parameters in the network and ensures that the model can detect the same feature (e.g., an edge or a corner) regardless of where it appears in the image. This property also helps CNNs generalize better and avoid overfitting, especially when working with large datasets.

3. Translation Invariance

Pooling layers, combined with the convolutional layers, give CNNs a form of **translation invariance**. This means that if an object appears in different locations in an image, the CNN can still recognize it because the convolution and pooling operations help the model focus on the presence of features rather than their specific locations. This makes CNNs highly effective for tasks like object detection, where the object might appear at varying locations in the image.

4. Hierarchical Feature Learning

CNNs excel at learning hierarchical features. Early layers in the network learn to detect low-level features such as edges and textures, while deeper layers learn more complex features, such as shapes, patterns, and objects. This hierarchical feature learning is what allows CNNs to recognize complex objects and scenes with high accuracy, making them indispensable for image classification and recognition tasks.

5. Efficient Parameterization

Unlike traditional fully connected neural networks, which require a large number of parameters due to the need to connect each input neuron to every output neuron, CNNs dramatically reduce the number of parameters through the use of filters and weight sharing. This makes them more computationally efficient and scalable, even for large image datasets.

Key Applications of CNNs in Image Data

CNNs have been successfully applied to a wide variety of image-based tasks. Some of the most common and impactful applications include:

1. Image Classification

In image classification, the task is to assign a label to an entire image. CNNs excel in this domain because of their ability to learn both low-level and high-level features in images. Common datasets used for training image classification models include **CIFAR-10, ImageNet**, and **MNIST**.

2. Object Detection

Object detection involves not only classifying the object in an image but also locating it by drawing bounding boxes around the detected objects. CNNs, along with architectures like **R-CNN** and **YOLO (You Only Look Once)**, have made significant advancements in real-time object detection tasks.

3. Semantic Segmentation

Semantic segmentation is the process of classifying each pixel in an image into one of several predefined categories. This is useful for tasks like medical image analysis, where each part of an image needs to be labeled (e.g., tumors, organs). CNNs, particularly **Fully Convolutional Networks (FCNs)**, have revolutionized segmentation tasks.

4. Face Recognition

CNNs are used extensively in face recognition tasks, where the goal is to identify or verify individuals based on facial features. They are capable of learning fine-grained details that are essential for distinguishing between different faces in images.

5. Style Transfer and Image Generation

CNNs, combined with other deep learning techniques, have been used in **style transfer** (transferring the artistic style of one image to another) and **generative models** (creating entirely new images based on learned features). Architectures like **Generative Adversarial Networks (GANs)** also leverage CNNs to generate realistic images from random noise.

Convolutional Neural Networks (CNNs) are a powerful tool for processing image data, owing to their ability to learn hierarchical features, maintain spatial relationships, and reduce computational complexity through weight sharing and pooling operations. By focusing on local features, CNNs are able to recognize objects, patterns, and structures in images with remarkable accuracy. The combination of convolutional layers, activation functions, pooling, and fully connected layers makes CNNs the go-to solution for a wide range of image-based tasks, from classification to detection and segmentation.

As we continue to explore deeper aspects of CNNs in later chapters, you'll see how these fundamental concepts are applied in real-world scenarios, and how you can implement your own CNNs for complex image processing tasks.

Layers in CNNs: Convolutional, Pooling, and Fully Connected Layers

In a Convolutional Neural Network (CNN), the architecture is designed to process visual data by extracting features at various levels of detail, from simple edges to complex textures and object parts. The layers within a CNN each play a unique role in the feature extraction and classification process. Understanding the purpose and function of each type of layer—**convolutional layers, pooling layers, and fully connected layers**—is essential to grasping how CNNs operate on image data.

Convolutional Layers: The Core Feature Extractors

The **convolutional layer** is the foundation of any CNN and is specifically designed to handle the spatial relationships in image data. This layer applies a series of filters (also called kernels) across the image to extract specific features, such as edges, textures, or shapes. Each convolutional layer in a CNN learns multiple filters that represent distinct features in the input images, from low-level characteristics in the first layers to more abstract concepts in deeper layers.

How Convolutional Layers Work

1. **Filters (Kernels)**: Filters are small matrices (often 3x3, 5x5, or 7x7) that slide over the image (or the output of a previous layer). At each position, the filter performs element-wise multiplication with the image pixels and sums the results to produce a single value for that region. This operation is called a **convolution**.

2. **Feature Maps**: As the filter slides across the entire image, it generates a new matrix called a **feature map**. Each feature map highlights specific aspects of the image based on the filter's characteristics. For example, one filter might detect vertical edges, while another detects diagonal edges.

3. **Stride and Padding**: The **stride** determines how far the filter moves across the image at each step. A stride of 1 means the filter moves one pixel at a time, while a stride of 2 means it moves two pixels at a time. **Padding** involves adding extra pixels (usually zeroes) around the image border to ensure that the filter covers the entire image and that the resulting feature map has the same dimensions as the input.

Why Convolutional Layers Are Essential in CNNs

Convolutional layers are uniquely suited for processing images because they capture **local patterns** in the data. Each filter focuses on specific regions of the image, allowing CNNs to preserve the spatial structure of the image while highlighting important features. Additionally, convolutional layers drastically reduce the number of parameters needed compared to fully connected layers, making them more computationally efficient and scalable.

Pooling Layers: Reducing Dimensionality and Enhancing Robustness

Pooling layers follow convolutional layers and serve to reduce the spatial dimensions of the feature maps, helping to control overfitting and reduce computational load. Pooling layers achieve this by summarizing small patches in the feature maps, allowing the network to become more **invariant to small shifts and distortions** in the image.

Types of Pooling

1. **Max Pooling**: The most common pooling operation in CNNs, max pooling takes the maximum value from a small window (usually 2x2 or 3x3) in each feature map. By selecting the strongest feature (the maximum value) in each region, max pooling emphasizes prominent features and reduces the dimensions of the feature map.
2. **Average Pooling**: In average pooling, the average value within each window is calculated instead of the maximum. While this method is less commonly used, it can be beneficial in certain applications where a smoother, more generalized representation of features is desirable.
3. **Global Pooling**: Global pooling, such as **global max pooling** or **global average pooling**, takes the maximum or average of the entire feature map instead of a local region. This is often used to further reduce the dimensions before passing the features to fully connected layers, especially in deeper networks.

Benefits of Pooling Layers

Pooling layers reduce the number of parameters and computations in the network, making it more efficient. By summarizing regions of the feature map, pooling also introduces a degree of **translation invariance**, meaning that the model becomes less sensitive to small shifts, rotations, or distortions in the image. This helps the CNN generalize better across different images, even if they are not perfectly aligned.

Fully Connected Layers: Integrating Features for Classification

After passing through multiple convolutional and pooling layers, the high-level features extracted from the image are combined and interpreted by one or more **fully connected layers**. Fully connected layers play a crucial role in the final stages of the CNN, where they integrate the learned features into a decision about the input data, such as classifying an image into a specific category.

Function of Fully Connected Layers

1. **Flattening the Feature Maps**: Before connecting to a fully connected layer, the feature maps from the last pooling layer are **flattened** into a one-dimensional vector. Flattening converts the multi-dimensional feature maps into a single vector that can be fed into a fully connected layer.

2. **Connecting Neurons**: In fully connected layers, each neuron is connected to every neuron in the previous layer. This dense connection enables the network to learn complex patterns and interactions between features, allowing it to make decisions based on all the information extracted from the image.

3. **Final Classification Layer**: For classification tasks, the last fully connected layer is typically followed by an **activation function** like **softmax**, which converts the output into probabilities for each class. The class with the highest probability is chosen as the predicted class for the image.

Importance of Fully Connected Layers in CNNs

Fully connected layers combine the local features learned by the convolutional layers and aggregate them to make a final prediction. They bring together all the information gathered through convolutions and pooling, creating a high-level understanding of the image. By transforming the extracted features into meaningful predictions, fully connected layers play an essential role in tasks like image classification, object detection, and more.

Layer Interaction and the Hierarchical Feature Extraction Process

In a CNN, these layers—convolutional, pooling, and fully connected—work together in a structured hierarchy. Here's a typical flow:

1. **Convolutional Layers Extract Local Features**: Early layers use small filters to capture local features, such as edges or textures, in the image.
2. **Pooling Layers Reduce Dimensionality**: Pooling summarizes these features, creating a smaller, more abstract representation while maintaining the essential characteristics.
3. **Deeper Convolutional Layers Capture Complex Patterns**: As we progress through the network, deeper convolutional layers capture more complex and high-level patterns, like shapes or objects.
4. **Fully Connected Layers Integrate Features for Final Decisions**: The final fully connected layers combine all these learned features to make a prediction or classification.

This hierarchical approach to feature extraction makes CNNs extremely powerful for handling complex visual data, as each layer builds upon the previous ones to create increasingly detailed representations of the input image.

Convolutional Neural Networks rely on a well-organized structure of layers to effectively process and classify visual data. Convolutional layers act as the primary feature extractors, pooling layers simplify and reduce the spatial dimensions, and fully connected layers use the extracted features to make the final prediction. Together, these layers form a powerful model capable of handling a wide range of image-based tasks.

Common Architectures: Overview of LeNet, AlexNet, VGG, and ResNet

Convolutional Neural Networks (CNNs) have evolved through various architectures over the years, each one pushing the boundaries of performance and efficiency in handling complex image recognition tasks. Some of the most influential architectures—**LeNet, AlexNet, VGG, and ResNet**—have set new standards and introduced foundational principles in deep learning. Here, we'll review each architecture, highlighting its contributions, design principles, and impact on CNN development.

LeNet: The Pioneer in Convolutional Networks

Developed by: Yann LeCun and colleagues in the late 1980s and early 1990s

Use Case: Handwritten digit recognition (notably used for MNIST dataset)

Overview of LeNet

LeNet was one of the first CNN architectures designed specifically for image processing tasks, particularly for recognizing handwritten characters. This architecture laid the foundation for modern CNNs by introducing core principles such as convolutional and pooling layers to reduce the need for complex preprocessing of image data.

Structure of LeNet

- **Input Layer**: The input to LeNet is a grayscale image, typically 32x32 pixels.
- **Convolutional Layers**: LeNet has two convolutional layers. Each is followed by a pooling layer to reduce spatial dimensions, helping the model generalize better.
- **Fully Connected Layers**: After feature extraction, LeNet uses two fully connected layers to interpret and classify the features.
- **Output Layer**: The output layer provides classification probabilities for the target classes.

Impact and Limitations

LeNet is simple and computationally efficient, making it highly suitable for early image processing tasks. While it performs well on small datasets, LeNet's simplicity limits its scalability and effectiveness on complex datasets or color images.

AlexNet: CNN Breakthrough in Large-Scale Image Recognition

Developed by: Alex Krizhevsky, Ilya Sutskever, and Geoffrey Hinton in 2012

Use Case: Large-scale image classification (e.g., ImageNet dataset)

Overview of AlexNet

AlexNet marked a major breakthrough in CNN development by achieving unprecedented performance on the ImageNet Large Scale Visual Recognition Challenge (ILSVRC) in 2012. AlexNet demonstrated the effectiveness of deep CNNs and was a catalyst for the surge in interest and development in deep learning.

Structure of AlexNet

- **Input Layer**: AlexNet takes 224x224 RGB images, enabling it to handle more complex and realistic datasets.
- **Convolutional Layers**: AlexNet consists of five convolutional layers, with some followed by max-pooling layers. AlexNet also introduced **overlapping pooling** (using slightly larger pooling windows with smaller strides), which helped improve performance.
- **ReLU Activation**: AlexNet was one of the first architectures to popularize the use of **ReLU** (Rectified Linear Unit) as an activation function, which accelerates training compared to traditional activation functions like sigmoid or tanh.
- **Fully Connected Layers**: Three fully connected layers are included, with a softmax activation at the end for classification.
- **Dropout Regularization**: AlexNet used dropout to prevent overfitting by randomly deactivating neurons during training, which was a significant innovation at the time.

Impact

AlexNet demonstrated that deep CNNs could outperform traditional methods when combined with sufficient computational power (in AlexNet's case, GPUs). It set a new standard for deep learning architectures, inspiring subsequent developments in CNN design.

VGG: Going Deeper with Smaller Kernels

Developed by: Visual Geometry Group (VGG) at the University of Oxford in 2014

Use Case: General-purpose image classification (also popular on ImageNet dataset)

Overview of VGG

VGG emphasized the importance of depth in CNNs, showing that increasing the number of layers could lead to better performance, provided the architecture was carefully designed. The VGG model architecture is known for using **small 3x3 convolution filters**, stacked to create deep networks with up to 19 layers.

Structure of VGG

- **Input Layer**: VGG takes 224x224 RGB images, similar to AlexNet.
- **Convolutional Layers**: VGG architectures are deeper than previous networks, typically containing 16 or 19 layers. Each convolutional layer uses 3x3 filters with a stride of 1, providing a balance between model complexity and computational efficiency.
- **Max Pooling Layers**: After every few convolutional layers, VGG applies max pooling to reduce the spatial dimensions.
- **Fully Connected Layers**: VGG includes two or three fully connected layers at the end of the network for classification.
- **Softmax Layer**: The final output layer uses softmax activation to classify images into the desired number of categories.

Impact and Limitations

The simplicity and uniformity of VGG's design make it easy to understand

and implement, and the model performs well on a range of tasks. However, the architecture is computationally intensive and requires a significant amount of memory and storage, making it challenging to deploy in resource-limited environments.

ResNet: Solving the Depth Problem with Skip Connections

Developed by: Kaiming He and colleagues at Microsoft Research in 2015

Use Case: Complex image classification and other computer vision tasks (highly successful on ImageNet and other benchmarks)

Overview of ResNet

ResNet (Residual Network) introduced a groundbreaking innovation with **skip connections** (or residual connections), allowing extremely deep networks (over 100 layers) to be trained effectively. ResNet's innovation of **residual learning** addressed the problem of vanishing gradients, which often prevents very deep networks from converging during training.

Structure of ResNet

- **Input Layer**: ResNet can take a variety of input sizes but is commonly used with 224x224 RGB images.
- **Residual Blocks**: ResNet's architecture is built from **residual blocks**, each containing multiple convolutional layers. Within each residual block, a skip connection allows the input to bypass one or more layers and be added to the output of the block.
- **Skip Connections**: By bypassing certain layers, skip connections enable the network to learn **identity mappings**, making it easier to train deeper networks without suffering from degradation or vanishing gradients.
- **Bottleneck Layers**: For very deep architectures, ResNet employs bottleneck layers that use 1x1 convolutions to reduce the number of parameters, making the model more efficient.
- **Fully Connected Layer**: Similar to other CNN architectures, the final layer is a fully connected layer with softmax activation for classification.

Impact

ResNet achieved state-of-the-art results on the ImageNet dataset, proving that extremely deep networks could be effectively trained and outperform shallower architectures. The residual connections introduced by ResNet have since become a staple in deep learning, particularly in tasks requiring very deep models. ResNet's design principle also inspired various other architectures, such as DenseNet and EfficientNet.

- **LeNet**: Pioneered CNNs with simple layers, suitable for basic tasks like digit recognition.
- **AlexNet**: Popularized deeper CNNs and ReLU activation, demonstrating the power of CNNs on large-scale image data.
- **VGG**: Emphasized depth with small 3x3 filters, resulting in a very deep network architecture with uniform layers.
- **ResNet**: Introduced skip connections to address the vanishing gradient problem, enabling effective training of very deep networks.

Each of these architectures has made a unique contribution to the evolution of CNNs, expanding the possibilities for image recognition and other computer vision tasks. The progression from LeNet to ResNet highlights the increasing complexity and power of CNNs, culminating in architectures that can achieve remarkable accuracy and efficiency on challenging visual data. Understanding these foundational models provides insights into both the capabilities of CNNs and the design choices that drive their success.

Building an Image Classifier with CNNs: A Practical Guide

Developing an image classifier using Convolutional Neural Networks (CNNs) involves several essential steps, from data preparation to model architecture design, training, and evaluation. In this section, we'll build a CNN-based image classifier step-by-step, explaining key concepts along the way. For our example, we'll work on a simple dataset like CIFAR-

10, which contains labeled images across ten different classes, making it a suitable dataset for beginners. This process can be applied to other image classification tasks with minimal adjustments.

Step 1: Preparing the Dataset

Before building the CNN model, we need a labeled dataset that our model can learn from. In our example, we'll use CIFAR-10, but you can adapt the following steps to other datasets, such as MNIST or custom datasets.

Dataset Loading and Inspection:

- Using popular libraries like TensorFlow or PyTorch, load the CIFAR-10 dataset.
- Inspect a few images to understand the dataset's structure and verify that the classes are well-represented.

python

```
# Example with TensorFlow's Keras library
from tensorflow.keras.datasets import cifar10
(train_images, train_labels), (test_images, test_labels) =
cifar10.load_data()
```

Data Preprocessing:

- **Normalization**: Rescale the pixel values (typically ranging from 0 to 255) to a range of 0 to 1, which improves model convergence.
- **One-Hot Encoding**: Convert class labels into one-hot encoded vectors if required.

python

```
# Normalize the images
train_images, test_images = train_images / 255.0, test_images /
255.0
```

Data Augmentation (Optional):

- To make the model more robust and prevent overfitting, apply transformations like random rotations, flips, or zooms to artificially expand the dataset. TensorFlow's ImageDataGenerator or PyTorch's transforms can be used for this.

```python
from tensorflow.keras.preprocessing.image import
ImageDataGenerator
datagen = ImageDataGenerator(
    rotation_range=20,
    width_shift_range=0.2,
    height_shift_range=0.2,
    horizontal_flip=True
)
datagen.fit(train_images)
```

Step 2: Designing the CNN Architecture

When designing a CNN for image classification, a straightforward architecture typically includes a sequence of convolutional, pooling, and fully connected layers.

1. **Convolutional Layer**: Applies multiple filters to capture local patterns like edges and textures.
2. **Pooling Layer**: Reduces the spatial dimensions, preserving essential information while decreasing computation.
3. **Fully Connected Layer**: Flattens the features from convolutional layers into a 1D array for classification.

Example CNN Architecture

Let's design a CNN with three convolutional blocks, followed by fully connected layers. This architecture strikes a balance between simplicity and accuracy for a dataset like CIFAR-10.

python

```python
from tensorflow.keras.models import Sequential
from tensorflow.keras.layers import Conv2D, MaxPooling2D,
Flatten, Dense, Dropout

model = Sequential([
    # First Convolutional Block
    Conv2D(32, (3, 3), activation='relu', input_shape=(32, 32,
    3)),
    MaxPooling2D((2, 2)),

    # Second Convolutional Block
    Conv2D(64, (3, 3), activation='relu'),
    MaxPooling2D((2, 2)),

    # Third Convolutional Block
    Conv2D(128, (3, 3), activation='relu'),
    MaxPooling2D((2, 2)),

    # Flattening and Fully Connected Layers
    Flatten(),
    Dense(128, activation='relu'),
    Dropout(0.5),  # Prevents overfitting
    Dense(10, activation='softmax')  # Output layer with 10
    classes
])
```

Step 3: Compiling the Model

To train the CNN model, we need to compile it by specifying:

- **Loss Function**: sparse_categorical_crossentropy for multi-class classification.

- **Optimizer**: Adam or SGD for adjusting the model weights.
- **Metrics**: accuracy to monitor performance.

```python
model.compile(optimizer='adam',
              loss='sparse_categorical_crossentropy',
              metrics=['accuracy'])
```

Step 4: Training the Model

Training the CNN involves feeding the model with training data in batches, iteratively adjusting weights based on errors calculated through the loss function.

Fit the Model: Specify the number of epochs and batch size. Using validation data helps monitor model performance and adjust if overfitting is detected.

```python
history = model.fit(datagen.flow(train_images, train_labels,
batch_size=32),
                    epochs=25,
                    validation_data=(test_images, test_labels))
```

Training Visualization (Optional): Track the model's performance with visualizations of accuracy and loss over epochs.

```python
import matplotlib.pyplot as plt

plt.plot(history.history['accuracy'], label='accuracy')
plt.plot(history.history['val_accuracy'], label='val_accuracy')
plt.xlabel('Epoch')
```

```
plt.ylabel('Accuracy')
plt.legend(loc='lower right')
plt.show()
```

Step 5: Evaluating the Model

After training, evaluate the model on the test dataset to gauge its generalization capabilities.

python

```
test_loss, test_acc = model.evaluate(test_images, test_labels)
print(f"Test accuracy: {test_acc}")
```

Step 6: Fine-Tuning and Optimization

To improve model accuracy, consider:

- **Hyperparameter Tuning**: Adjusting learning rate, batch size, and architecture complexity.
- **Regularization**: Techniques like dropout or L2 regularization help prevent overfitting.
- **Data Augmentation**: Using transformations if the model shows signs of overfitting.

Building an image classifier with CNNs involves methodical steps: data preparation, model architecture design, training, evaluation, and optimization. This foundational understanding equips you to adapt and scale CNNs for a wide variety of image classification tasks, making the architecture flexible and powerful for real-world applications.

Hyperparameter Tuning in CNNs: Optimizing CNNs for Performance

Hyperparameter tuning is a crucial process in optimizing Convolutional Neural Networks (CNNs) to achieve higher accuracy and better generalization on unseen data. Tuning these hyperparameters—such as learning rate, batch size, number of filters, and regularization methods—can significantly impact the model's performance and efficiency.

This section delves into essential hyperparameters for CNNs, their effects, and strategies for tuning them effectively.

Key Hyperparameters in CNNs

1. **Learning Rate**: The learning rate controls how much the model's weights are adjusted with each iteration. A learning rate that's too high may cause the model to converge too quickly to a suboptimal solution, while a learning rate that's too low can result in slow training or getting stuck in local minima.

2. **Batch Size**: Batch size determines the number of samples processed before the model updates its parameters. Smaller batch sizes introduce more variability in gradient estimates, which can help escape local minima, but larger batch sizes can lead to more stable and efficient training.

3. **Number of Epochs**: This defines how many times the model will iterate through the entire training dataset. Insufficient epochs can lead to underfitting, while too many can lead to overfitting.

4. **Filter Count and Size**: The number of filters in each convolutional layer impacts the model's capacity to detect features. Generally, more filters allow for more complex representations, but they also increase the computational cost. Filter size (e.g., 3x3, 5x5) affects the receptive field, with smaller filters focusing on local details and larger filters capturing broader context.

5. **Pooling Size**: Pooling layers reduce the spatial dimensions, and the pool size (e.g., 2x2) impacts the amount of information retained. Larger pooling sizes reduce dimensions more aggressively but may lose finer details.

6. **Regularization Methods**:

- **Dropout Rate**: Dropout helps prevent overfitting by randomly setting a fraction of units to zero during training. Tuning the dropout rate is essential for balancing model complexity and generalization.

- **L2 Regularization**: Adds a penalty proportional to the squared value of the weights, discouraging overly large weights and thus helping prevent overfitting.

Strategies for Hyperparameter Tuning

Grid Search: Grid search exhaustively explores a predefined set of hyperparameters. For example, if you're unsure whether a learning rate of 0.001 or 0.0001 will perform better, you can try both values. While grid search is simple to implement, it's computationally expensive since it tests every combination.

```python

from sklearn.model_selection import GridSearchCV
```

Random Search: Instead of trying every combination, random search samples random combinations of hyperparameters within specified ranges. This approach is often more efficient than grid search, especially for high-dimensional search spaces.

```python

from sklearn.model_selection import RandomizedSearchCV
```

Bayesian Optimization: Bayesian optimization builds a probabilistic model to predict which hyperparameter combinations are likely to perform well, guiding the search more intelligently. Libraries like scikit-optimize or Hyperopt can be used to perform Bayesian optimization.

Learning Rate Schedulers: Instead of tuning a fixed learning rate, you can use a learning rate scheduler, which adjusts the learning rate dynamically. For example, ReduceLROnPlateau decreases the learning rate when the model's performance stops improving, while a cyclical learning rate schedule varies the learning rate cyclically over training.

```python
from tensorflow.keras.callbacks import ReduceLROnPlateau

lr_scheduler = ReduceLROnPlateau(monitor='val_loss', factor=0.5,
patience=3)
```

Early Stopping: Early stopping monitors validation performance and halts training when it no longer improves. This prevents overfitting and reduces training time by stopping the process as soon as the model starts to overfit.

```python
from tensorflow.keras.callbacks import EarlyStopping

early_stopping = EarlyStopping(monitor='val_loss', patience=5)
```

Practical Tips for CNN Hyperparameter Tuning

1. **Tune Learning Rate First**: The learning rate is often the most sensitive hyperparameter, so it's beneficial to adjust it early on. A learning rate finder, available in some libraries, can help identify an appropriate range.
2. **Batch Size and Learning Rate**: These two parameters are often interdependent. Larger batch sizes allow for higher learning rates, while smaller batch sizes might require lower learning rates to prevent oscillations in the training process.
3. **Experiment with Filter Counts and Architectures**: Explore the number of filters in each layer, as well as the arrangement of layers. For instance, stacking more convolutional layers with fewer filters can sometimes capture more granular patterns without a drastic increase in computational cost.

4. **Utilize Transfer Learning When Possible**: Instead of building a CNN from scratch, fine-tuning a pre-trained model (e.g., VGG or ResNet) on your specific dataset can save time and often yields better results, especially if you have limited data.

5. **Use Dropout and Batch Normalization Judiciously**: Applying dropout before the fully connected layers and using batch normalization in convolutional layers can stabilize training and reduce overfitting. However, excessive dropout can hinder model learning, so adjust the dropout rate carefully.

Hyperparameter tuning in CNNs is essential for achieving optimal performance and balancing accuracy, training time, and computational efficiency.

Recurrent Neural Networks (RNNs) and Sequence Modeling

What Are RNNs? Introduction to RNNs and Sequence Data Recurrent Neural Networks (RNNs) are a class of artificial neural networks specifically designed to process sequential data, where the order and context of the information matter. Unlike traditional feedforward neural networks, RNNs contain recurrent connections that allow information to persist, effectively making them well-suited for tasks involving time-series, text, audio, and other types of sequence data.

Understanding RNNs and their unique structure is essential for anyone working with data where the sequence is critical, such as in natural language processing (NLP), speech recognition, and financial forecasting.

Key Concepts Behind RNNs

In a standard neural network, data flows in a single direction from input to output without any concept of time or sequence. RNNs, however, incorporate a looping mechanism that enables the network to carry information across steps in a sequence. This ability to maintain context over time steps is what differentiates RNNs and makes them powerful for sequence modeling.

Sequential Data:

- Sequential data has an inherent order in which each element depends on the previous one, making it essential to preserve this temporal relationship. Examples include stock prices over days, a sequence of words in a sentence, or audio signals where each sound frequency depends on the previous and subsequent sounds.

- RNNs capture these dependencies, which helps them understand and predict sequence patterns.

Recurrence and Memory:

- The recurrence in RNNs allows them to have memory, enabling them to leverage information from previous steps in the sequence. This memory is created through feedback loops where information from the previous time step is fed back into the network.
- At each time step, the RNN updates its hidden state based on the current input and the previous hidden state, effectively storing contextual information.

The Structure of RNNs:

- RNNs have a chain-like structure, where each "cell" or "unit" in the sequence passes information to the next. In other words, each time step has a recurrent cell that takes in the current input and a hidden state from the previous cell, processes them, and then outputs a new hidden state for the next cell in the sequence.
- This structure allows the RNN to "remember" information from earlier steps in the sequence, making it effective for capturing dependencies.

Mathematically, this process is represented as:

$$h_t = f(W_x \cdot x_t + W_h \cdot h_{t-1} + b)$$

Here:

- h_t is the hidden state at time step t.
- W_x and W_h are the weights for the input and hidden state, respectively.
- x_t is the input at time step t.
- b is the bias term.
- f is an activation function, typically a tanh or ReLU function.

Types of Sequential Data RNNs Handle

RNNs are widely used for various types of sequence data. Here are a few major applications:

Text Data:

- In text processing tasks, each word in a sentence is dependent on previous words, as they establish context and meaning. RNNs capture these dependencies, making them valuable in NLP tasks such as language translation, text generation, and sentiment analysis.

Time-Series Data:

- RNNs are highly effective for time-series data, where patterns evolve over time. Examples include stock price predictions, weather forecasting, and sensor data analysis. By capturing trends and seasonality, RNNs can model and predict future values based on historical data.

Audio and Speech Data:

- Audio data is another sequence where each time step (or frequency component) is influenced by the previous ones. RNNs are effective for speech recognition and audio analysis because they can interpret the sequence and maintain the flow of spoken language.

Video Data:

- Video frames are sequentially organized, making RNNs useful in video analysis and captioning. Each frame in a video has temporal relevance to the ones before and after it, so RNNs can help capture the progression of movement or scenes.

RNN Workflow: An Overview

The workflow of an RNN involves processing each element in the sequence step by step, updating its hidden state with each new piece of data.

Input Processing:

- Each element in the input sequence is fed into the RNN one at a time. For example, in a sentence, each word is represented as a vector, and each word vector is fed into the RNN in sequence.

Hidden State Update:

- For each time step, the RNN takes the current input and the previous hidden state to produce an updated hidden state. This hidden state carries contextual information from previous time steps and is used to influence future predictions.

Output Generation:

- Depending on the type of RNN model, an output can be generated at each time step or only at the end of the sequence. For example, in language translation, each word might produce an output word, whereas in time-series prediction, only the final step may produce the output.

Limitations of Basic RNNs

While RNNs have great potential for sequence modeling, they also have notable limitations, primarily due to the challenge of maintaining long-term dependencies.

Vanishing and Exploding Gradients:

- In practice, training RNNs over long sequences can lead to issues with vanishing or exploding gradients. This occurs when gradients diminish (vanishing) or grow uncontrollably (exploding) during backpropagation through time, making it difficult for the network to learn long-term dependencies.

Difficulty in Learning Long-Term Dependencies:

- RNNs struggle to retain information from earlier time steps over long sequences, leading to degraded performance on tasks requiring long-term memory. For example, remembering the context of a sentence from several words back may be challenging for basic RNNs.

Computationally Intensive:

- Due to their sequential nature, RNNs can be computationally expensive to train, as they cannot easily parallelize processing across time steps. Each time step must be processed in sequence, which can slow down training for long input sequences.

Solutions and Alternatives: LSTM and GRU

To overcome some of the limitations of basic RNNs, specialized variants like Long Short-Term Memory (LSTM) networks and Gated Recurrent Units (GRUs) have been developed. These models incorporate gating mechanisms to better handle long-term dependencies.

Long Short-Term Memory (LSTM):

- LSTMs include memory cells that can retain information for longer periods, along with gates (input, forget, and output) that control the flow of information. These gates help the network decide which information to keep, forget, or output, thereby addressing the vanishing gradient problem and enabling the model to capture long-term dependencies more effectively.

Gated Recurrent Unit (GRU):

- GRUs are a simpler and computationally efficient alternative to LSTMs. They combine the forget and input gates into a single update gate, which reduces the model's complexity and training time while still effectively capturing dependencies in sequence data.

RNNs are a powerful tool for modeling sequential data, capturing dependencies, and maintaining context through their recurrent connections. Despite the limitations of basic RNNs, these networks form the backbone of many sequence-processing tasks across fields like NLP, time-series forecasting, and speech recognition. With the development of advanced variants like LSTMs and GRUs, RNN-based models have become even more adept at handling complex, long-term dependencies, broadening their applicability in real-world tasks.

Variants of RNNs: LSTMs and GRUs, and Their Advantages in Handling Sequential Data

While Recurrent Neural Networks (RNNs) are highly effective for sequence data, basic RNNs often struggle with learning long-term dependencies due to issues like the vanishing gradient problem. This limitation can cause standard RNNs to lose context over long sequences, making it challenging to capture relationships in tasks requiring memory of past inputs over extended steps. To address these issues, more advanced RNN variants, such as Long Short-Term Memory (LSTM) networks and Gated Recurrent Units (GRUs), have been developed. These architectures incorporate gating mechanisms that allow the model to selectively retain or discard information, offering significant improvements in handling sequential data.

Long Short-Term Memory Networks (LSTMs)

Long Short-Term Memory (LSTM) networks were designed specifically to address the limitations of standard RNNs by improving memory retention and managing long-term dependencies within sequences. Introduced by Hochreiter and Schmidhuber in 1997, LSTMs use a unique gating mechanism that allows the model to control the flow of information, deciding which data to keep or discard as it processes each time step. This added control allows LSTMs to maintain relevant information over long sequences more effectively than traditional RNNs.

Core Components of LSTM Cells: Each LSTM cell contains three main gates that regulate the information within the cell: the forget gate, the input gate, and the output gate. These gates help the model selectively retain or discard information at each time step.

Forget Gate:

- The forget gate determines which information from the previous cell state should be discarded. It takes the current input and the previous hidden state as inputs, applies a sigmoid function to produce a value between 0 and 1, and multiplies this value with the cell state.
- Values close to 0 cause the information to be mostly forgotten, while values close to 1 retain the information.

Input Gate:

- The input gate decides which new information should be added to the cell state. It combines the current input and the previous hidden state, applies a sigmoid activation to determine the importance of the new information, and then applies a tanh activation to regulate the range of values.
- This combination allows the LSTM cell to add new, relevant information into the cell state.

Output Gate:

- The output gate determines what the next hidden state should be. It takes the updated cell state, applies a tanh function, and then multiplies it by the output gate's own sigmoid-regulated output.
- This hidden state is then passed to the next LSTM cell, carrying updated contextual information through the sequence.

The overall process allows the LSTM to manage and retain information effectively over long time sequences, making it highly suitable for tasks where distant dependencies exist, such as long text processing, language translation, and music generation.

Advantages of LSTMs:

- **Long-Term Memory Retention**: LSTMs can retain important information from earlier in the sequence for longer periods, which helps them capture long-term dependencies more effectively than basic RNNs.
- **Effective Gradient Flow**: By using gated mechanisms, LSTMs help mitigate the vanishing gradient problem, enabling more stable and effective learning over time.
- **Enhanced Contextual Understanding**: LSTMs are highly effective in understanding contextual information in complex sequences, making them well-suited for tasks such as language modeling and speech recognition.

Gated Recurrent Units (GRUs)

Gated Recurrent Units (GRUs), introduced by Cho et al. in 2014, are another RNN variant that addresses similar issues as LSTMs but with a more simplified structure. GRUs merge some of the gating functions found in LSTMs to create a less complex, more computationally efficient architecture. While LSTMs have three gates (forget, input, and output), GRUs use only two: the update gate and the reset gate. This simplification reduces the model's computational load, making GRUs faster to train while still performing well in tasks involving long-term dependencies.

Core Components of GRU Cells: The GRU cell has two main gates—the update gate and the reset gate—that control the flow of information in a way similar to LSTMs but with fewer operations.

Update Gate:

- The update gate is a combination of the forget and input gates in LSTMs. It decides how much of the previous hidden state's information to carry forward and how much new information to incorporate. This gate allows the GRU to retain useful information over time and is central to its memory mechanism.

Reset Gate:

- The reset gate determines how much of the previous hidden state to forget. If the reset gate is activated, the model forgets some of the prior information and only considers the current input, which is helpful in tasks where the model needs to reset its memory periodically, such as in sentence segmentation.

The architecture of GRUs allows them to perform similarly to LSTMs in terms of long-term dependency retention while being computationally more efficient due to fewer parameters and simplified operations.

Advantages of GRUs:

- **Simpler Architecture**: The two-gate structure of GRUs makes them computationally faster and easier to train compared to LSTMs.
- **Comparable Performance**: Despite their simpler structure, GRUs often perform similarly to LSTMs, especially in tasks where long-term dependencies are essential.
- **Efficient for Shorter Sequences**: GRUs tend to be more efficient in handling tasks where sequences are shorter, as they achieve comparable

results to LSTMs without the overhead of extra gates.

Choosing Between LSTMs and GRUs

Both LSTMs and GRUs excel in handling sequential data, and choosing between them often depends on the specific requirements of the task and the computational resources available:

- **Task Complexity**: For complex tasks with intricate long-term dependencies (e.g., language translation or sentiment analysis over long text), LSTMs are typically favored due to their more robust memory structure.
- **Computational Efficiency**: GRUs are more computationally efficient, making them preferable in environments where processing power or memory is limited.
- **Training Speed**: GRUs generally train faster than LSTMs due to their simplified structure, making them an attractive option for rapid prototyping and scenarios where training speed is critical.

In many cases, the choice may also come down to experimentation, as both models have demonstrated excellent performance across various sequence-based tasks.

LSTMs and GRUs represent key advancements in neural networks for sequence data, each offering unique benefits. LSTMs excel at retaining long-term dependencies in complex tasks due to their sophisticated gating mechanisms, making them well-suited for applications like language translation, time-series forecasting, and speech recognition. GRUs, with their simpler structure and faster training times, are effective in similar applications but are especially valuable in scenarios where computational resources are limited or shorter sequences are processed.

Hands-On: Building a Text Generator with RNNs

Text generation is a popular application of Recurrent Neural Networks (RNNs), as RNNs excel at processing and generating sequences. In this section, we'll create a simple text generation model using RNNs. This model will take an input text corpus, learn the patterns of the language, and then generate new text based on what it has learned. For simplicity, we'll use TensorFlow and Keras to build and train our RNN model.

Step 1: Import Libraries

To begin, ensure you have TensorFlow and other essential libraries installed.

```python
import tensorflow as tf
import numpy as np
import pandas as pd
import random
import string
from tensorflow.keras.models import Sequential
from tensorflow.keras.layers import LSTM, Dense, Embedding
from tensorflow.keras.preprocessing.sequence import pad_sequences
from tensorflow.keras.utils import to_categorical
```

Step 2: Prepare the Text Data

For this example, we'll use a small corpus. For larger projects, consider more extensive datasets like classic novels or song lyrics.

1. **Load the Text**: Load the dataset and preprocess it.
2. **Tokenization**: Split the text into sequences that the model will learn from.

Here's a simple example:

python

```python
# Sample text corpus
text = "In the vast fields of deep learning, machines learn
patterns and create novel output."

# Convert text to lowercase and remove punctuation for simplicity
text = text.lower().translate(str.maketrans('', '',
string.punctuation))

# Tokenize the text into words
words = text.split()
unique_words = sorted(list(set(words)))
word_index = {word: i for i, word in enumerate(unique_words, 1)}
index_word = {i: word for word, i in word_index.items()}

# Create sequences
sequences = []
for i in range(1, len(words)):
    seq = words[:i+1]
    encoded_seq = [word_index[word] for word in seq]
    sequences.append(encoded_seq)
```

Step 3: Pad the Sequences

We want all sequences to be of equal length, so we'll use padding.

python

```python
# Define the max length of sequences
max_seq_len = max(len(seq) for seq in sequences)

# Pad sequences to have the same length
sequences = pad_sequences(sequences, maxlen=max_seq_len,
padding='pre')
```

Step 4: Split Data into Features and Labels

Now, split the data into input features (X) and the target label (y).

160

```python
python
```

```python
# Separate features and target
X, y = sequences[:, :-1], sequences[:, -1]
y = to_categorical(y, num_classes=len(unique_words) + 1)
```

Step 5: Define the RNN Model

We'll use an LSTM-based model for our text generator. This model architecture includes an Embedding layer, an LSTM layer, and a Dense output layer with a softmax activation for generating probabilities for each word.

```python
python
```

```python
# Define model
model = Sequential([
    Embedding(input_dim=len(unique_words) + 1, output_dim=10,
    input_length=max_seq_len - 1),
    LSTM(50, return_sequences=True),
    LSTM(50),
    Dense(len(unique_words) + 1, activation='softmax')
])

model.compile(loss='categorical_crossentropy', optimizer='adam',
metrics=['accuracy'])
model.summary()
```

Step 6: Train the Model

Train the model on the sequences, which will help it learn the patterns in the text data.

```python
python
```

```python
# Train model
history = model.fit(X, y, epochs=100, verbose=1)
```

Step 7: Generate Text

Once the model is trained, it can generate new text. For this, we'll give it a starting word and let it predict the next word in the sequence repeatedly until we reach the desired output length.

```python
# Function to generate text
def generate_text(seed_text, next_words):
    for _ in range(next_words):
        token_list = [word_index[word] for word in
        seed_text.split() if word in word_index]
        token_list = pad_sequences([token_list],
        maxlen=max_seq_len - 1, padding='pre')
        predicted = model.predict(token_list, verbose=0)
        predicted_word = index_word[np.argmax(predicted)]
        seed_text += " " + predicted_word
    return seed_text

# Example generation
print(generate_text("In the vast fields", 10))
```

Explanation of Key Steps

1. **Embedding Layer**: This layer converts words into dense vectors, making it easier for the model to understand the relationships between words.
2. **LSTM Layers**: The LSTM layers capture sequential dependencies in the text, enabling the model to "remember" previous words when predicting the next.
3. **Dense Layer with Softmax**: The final Dense layer with softmax activation outputs a probability distribution, allowing the model to select the most likely next word.

This text generator provides a foundational approach to RNN-based text generation using a small sample corpus. By adjusting the corpus and fine-tuning parameters, you can generate text that more closely resembles the patterns within any given dataset.

Applications of RNNs: Time Series Analysis, Natural Language Processing, and Speech Recognition

Recurrent Neural Networks (RNNs) have reshaped how we approach tasks that involve sequential or time-dependent data. Unlike traditional neural networks, RNNs are well-suited for tasks where the order of the data matters, such as predicting future values in time series, understanding language patterns, and recognizing speech. Here, we'll dive into three of the most prominent applications of RNNs: time series analysis, natural language processing (NLP), and speech recognition.

1. Time Series Analysis

Time series data is a sequence of data points collected or recorded at specific time intervals, making it ideal for RNNs due to their ability to capture dependencies over time. Common time series applications include stock market predictions, weather forecasting, and anomaly detection in sensor data.

Use Case: Stock Market Prediction

- **Objective**: Predict future stock prices based on historical data.
- **How RNNs Help**: RNNs, particularly LSTMs and GRUs, can learn patterns in stock prices over time. By training on historical data, the network can predict the next day's price or trends over a longer period.
- **Example**: An RNN model might take daily stock prices for the last year as input and predict prices for the next few days. Using recurrent connections, the model remembers trends like seasonal cycles, volatility, and momentum.

Use Case: Weather Forecasting

- **Objective**: Predict weather conditions (e.g., temperature, precipitation) based on past weather data.

- **How RNNs Help**: RNNs model dependencies between historical weather patterns, such as seasonal trends, unusual weather events, and gradual climate shifts.
- **Example**: A network can be trained on temperature, humidity, and wind speed data collected over years to forecast daily or even hourly weather conditions.

Use Case: Anomaly Detection in IoT and Sensors

- **Objective**: Detect unusual patterns or malfunctions in real-time data from sensors (e.g., in manufacturing, healthcare, or energy sectors).
- **How RNNs Help**: By learning normal operating patterns, RNNs can flag deviations that may indicate equipment failure, cybersecurity threats, or medical emergencies.
- **Example**: An RNN can monitor power consumption in a factory, identifying spikes or drops that deviate from expected patterns and signaling maintenance needs or potential security breaches.

2. Natural Language Processing (NLP)

NLP encompasses a variety of tasks involving the understanding, generation, and transformation of human language. RNNs are highly effective in NLP because they process words sequentially, capturing contextual relationships and long-term dependencies within sentences and paragraphs. Applications in NLP include language translation, text generation, and sentiment analysis.

Use Case: Machine Translation

- **Objective**: Translate text from one language to another while preserving context and meaning.
- **How RNNs Help**: RNNs (especially when combined with attention mechanisms) can handle variable-length sequences and maintain context across long phrases. In translation, words are processed in sequence,

and RNNs can align words in one language with their counterparts in another.

- **Example**: Google Translate employs RNNs (along with other models) to translate sentences by encoding a source language and decoding it into the target language, achieving high-quality translations with complex sentence structures.

Use Case: Text Generation

- **Objective**: Generate coherent text based on a seed word or phrase.
- **How RNNs Help**: RNNs can predict the next word in a sequence based on previous words, allowing them to generate new text that follows learned language patterns.
- **Example**: Applications like chatbots and writing assistance tools use RNN-based text generation to suggest responses, compose emails, or even write stories in a chosen style.

Use Case: Sentiment Analysis

- **Objective**: Classify the sentiment (e.g., positive, negative, neutral) expressed in a text.
- **How RNNs Help**: RNNs capture nuances in the text, like sarcasm or compound sentiments, by understanding the context created by preceding words.
- **Example**: Social media platforms, movie reviews, and customer feedback systems use RNNs to analyze sentiment and categorize opinions, helping businesses understand consumer sentiment toward products and services.

3. Speech Recognition

Speech recognition converts spoken language into text, which is invaluable in voice-activated applications, accessibility tools, and customer service automation. RNNs are well-suited for this because spoken language is inherently sequential, with dependencies between sounds, syllables, and words.

Use Case: Voice-to-Text Transcription

- **Objective**: Convert spoken language into written text accurately.
- **How RNNs Help**: RNNs capture phonetic patterns and map them to corresponding text representations. Advanced architectures, such as sequence-to-sequence RNNs with attention, can handle speech with different accents, speeds, and inflections.
- **Example**: Services like Google Voice Typing and Apple's Siri use RNN-based models to transcribe spoken words into text in real time.

Use Case: Virtual Assistants

- **Objective**: Understand voice commands and execute tasks or provide answers.
- **How RNNs Help**: Virtual assistants use RNNs to process voice input and generate an appropriate response. The model translates spoken input into text, which is then interpreted to generate relevant responses.
- **Example**: Virtual assistants like Alexa and Google Assistant use RNNs to enable users to control smart devices, search for information, or perform tasks like setting reminders and sending messages.

Use Case: Speaker Identification

- **Objective**: Identify individuals based on their voice characteristics.
- **How RNNs Help**: RNNs can analyze unique patterns in an individual's speech, such as tone, pitch, and rhythm. This capability is useful in security applications and personalized systems.
- **Example**: RNNs enable systems to recognize authorized users by voice, ensuring secure access to voice-activated accounts, and facilitating personalized user experiences by adapting responses to known users.

RNNs are foundational tools in AI applications involving sequential data. Their versatility in time series analysis, natural language processing, and speech recognition has led to widespread adoption across industries. Whether it's predicting stock prices, translating languages, or powering virtual assistants, RNNs continue to expand the boundaries of what's possible with AI.

Advanced Architectures and Techniques

I ntroduction to Transfer Learning: Concept and Benefits
Transfer learning is a powerful and increasingly popular technique
in deep learning that enables models to leverage the knowledge gained
from one task to improve performance on another related task. This
approach is especially valuable when labeled data is limited, computational
resources are constrained, or when you want to achieve high performance
with minimal retraining.

In traditional deep learning, models are trained from scratch, meaning
they begin with no prior knowledge and must learn all features from the
provided dataset. However, training models from scratch can be both time-
consuming and computationally expensive, often requiring large amounts
of labeled data. Transfer learning provides an alternative by allowing a
model to "transfer" the insights it gained from solving one task (typically
one with a large dataset) to another task, even if the second dataset is smaller.

What is Transfer Learning?

Transfer learning is the process of taking a pre-trained model—one that
has already been trained on a large, general dataset—and reusing it as the
starting point for a new, more specific task. Instead of training a deep neural
network from scratch, transfer learning leverages the patterns learned by an
existing model on a large dataset and applies them to a different, typically
smaller, dataset. This approach reduces the training time significantly and
can improve model performance.

In technical terms, transfer learning involves:

1. **Using a Pre-Trained Model**: Selecting a model that has already been trained on a large-scale, similar dataset (e.g., ImageNet for image-based tasks).
2. **Freezing Initial Layers**: Retaining the earlier layers of the pre-trained model, which often capture generic features (such as edges, textures, and shapes in images).
3. **Fine-Tuning**: Modifying and retraining the later layers on the new dataset to adapt the model to the specific features of the new task.

How Does Transfer Learning Work?

In deep neural networks, the layers closer to the input layer generally capture low-level, generic features (e.g., edges in images or basic word patterns in text). The deeper layers closer to the output layer capture high-level, more task-specific features. For transfer learning, the idea is to keep the generic layers unchanged since these low-level features are often useful across multiple tasks, while adapting or retraining the higher-level layers to specialize in the new task.

For example:

1. **Feature Extraction**: The lower layers of a pre-trained convolutional neural network (CNN) trained on a general dataset (such as ImageNet) might identify basic shapes and edges in an image. These features are generic enough to be useful in many image-based tasks.
2. **Task-Specific Learning**: By only updating the final layers, the model can adapt to detect task-specific features (like identifying disease markers in medical images or recognizing new categories of objects).

Benefits of Transfer Learning

Transfer learning offers several significant benefits in machine learning and deep learning workflows:

1. **Reduced Training Time**: Because the pre-trained model has already learned useful features, training can start from an advanced baseline.

This means fewer training epochs and, as a result, lower computational costs.

2. **Improved Performance with Limited Data**: When data is scarce, training a model from scratch can lead to poor generalization due to overfitting. Transfer learning allows models to leverage pre-learned features, often achieving higher accuracy and better generalization even on small datasets.

3. **Enhanced Performance on Complex Tasks**: Some tasks are challenging to learn from scratch due to high variability or noise in the data. Transfer learning enables the model to begin with more structured feature representations, increasing the likelihood of capturing complex patterns.

4. **Resource Efficiency**: For organizations and researchers with limited computational resources, transfer learning provides a practical way to deploy high-performing models without needing extensive computing power or access to large datasets.

5. **Broader Applicability**: Models developed using transfer learning can be adapted to a wide range of applications beyond their original purpose. For example, a CNN trained on ImageNet for general object recognition can be adapted for specialized fields, such as medical imaging, satellite data analysis, or industrial quality control.

Types of Transfer Learning

Transfer learning is applied in different ways depending on the task and the similarity between the source and target domains. Here are three common types:

1. **Domain Adaptation**: When there are similarities between the source and target domains but with different distributions (e.g., using a model trained on natural images for medical images), domain adaptation techniques can be used to adjust the pre-trained model for the target domain.

2. **Fine-Tuning**: In fine-tuning, a pre-trained model is partially or fully

retrained on the new task, with special attention given to the final layers to specialize in the new dataset. Fine-tuning is commonly used when the new task is similar to the original task, but has specific variations.

3. **Few-Shot Learning**: Few-shot learning is a form of transfer learning where the model is expected to generalize to the target task with very few examples. Pre-trained models are highly advantageous for few-shot learning, as they can adapt quickly with minimal labeled data in the new task.

Transfer Learning in Practice: Common Scenarios and Examples
Image Classification:

- **Scenario**: Suppose you want to build a model to classify different types of plants, but only have a limited dataset.
- **Solution**: Use a pre-trained model like ResNet or VGG, which has already learned to recognize a wide array of visual features. Fine-tune the last few layers on the plant dataset to make it a specialized plant classifier.

Object Detection in Medical Imaging:

- **Scenario**: A medical researcher wants to create a model to detect abnormalities in MRI scans, but lacks a large dataset.
- **Solution**: Start with a CNN pre-trained on ImageNet, which has learned foundational image recognition features. After freezing the early layers, the researcher can fine-tune the model on the medical imaging data, allowing it to learn medical-specific features for anomaly detection.

Natural Language Processing (NLP):

- **Scenario**: You want to develop a sentiment analysis model but have limited labeled text data.

- **Solution**: Use a language model like BERT or GPT, which has been pre-trained on vast amounts of text. Fine-tune the model on your sentiment analysis dataset. The model's understanding of language nuances will transfer to your dataset, requiring minimal additional training.

Limitations and Considerations

While transfer learning offers many benefits, it is essential to consider its limitations and potential pitfalls:

1. **Domain Mismatch**: If the source and target domains are too different, transfer learning may not yield meaningful results. For instance, using a model trained on natural images to classify microscopic cell images may require extensive fine-tuning.
2. **Risk of Overfitting**: If the target dataset is too small, overfitting can occur even with transfer learning. Regularization techniques like dropout, and using only the essential number of trainable layers, can help mitigate this risk.
3. **Computational Resources for Fine-Tuning**: Although transfer learning reduces the training time overall, fine-tuning large models, such as deep CNNs or transformer-based NLP models, still requires considerable resources. It is often best to experiment with how many layers need fine-tuning to balance performance and efficiency.
4. **Knowledge Distillation**: Sometimes, the pre-trained model may be too large to deploy in real-time applications. Techniques such as model compression and knowledge distillation (where a smaller "student" model learns from a larger "teacher" model) can be applied to make deployment more feasible.

Transfer learning is a transformative approach in deep learning, enabling models to achieve high accuracy with less data and reduced training time. By leveraging knowledge gained from large datasets, transfer learning allows models to generalize better on specific, often smaller datasets, making it especially valuable in real-world applications where labeled data is limited. Through techniques like fine-tuning and domain adaptation, transfer learning allows practitioners to create specialized models in fields ranging from computer vision to natural language processing and beyond.

Working with Pre-trained Models: Fine-tuning VGG, ResNet, or Inception for Custom Applications

Pre-trained models, particularly well-known architectures like VGG, ResNet, and Inception, have revolutionized deep learning by allowing practitioners to use powerful, well-tuned networks as a foundation for their own tasks. These models are typically trained on large datasets like ImageNet, which contains millions of images across thousands of categories. As a result, they excel at general image feature recognition and can often be adapted, or fine-tuned, to perform well on specific tasks with comparatively little additional training.

Fine-tuning a pre-trained model for a custom application involves several key steps: selecting the right model for the job, configuring the model layers to optimize for the new task, and training the model on the specific dataset to learn task-relevant features while retaining the original model's valuable feature representations. Below, we'll discuss how to approach fine-tuning with three popular models—VGG, ResNet, and Inception—and the best practices for adapting these architectures.

1. Choosing the Right Pre-trained Model: VGG, ResNet, or Inception

Each pre-trained model has unique characteristics suited for specific types of tasks. Here's a quick overview of each:

- **VGG (Visual Geometry Group)**: VGG is known for its simplicity and straightforward architecture, with several blocks of convolutional layers followed by fully connected layers. This model is effective when a straightforward, deep network is beneficial, especially for tasks where spatial hierarchies in images (like shapes and patterns) are important.
- **ResNet (Residual Network)**: ResNet introduced "skip connections,"

allowing the network to bypass certain layers during training. This architecture is advantageous for tasks requiring very deep networks, as it avoids the vanishing gradient problem and enables the network to learn complex hierarchies. ResNet models are suitable for tasks that require understanding of fine, deep-layered features.

- **Inception**: The Inception model (or GoogLeNet) uses a more complex architecture with multi-level feature extraction in each layer (via inception modules). This model captures features at different scales, making it particularly effective for images with complex or varied detail. Inception works well in applications needing multi-scale feature analysis, such as satellite imaging or medical imaging.

2. Setting Up the Model for Fine-Tuning

When adapting any pre-trained model, it's essential to configure the layers to suit your custom application. Fine-tuning generally involves freezing the early layers of the network, which capture low-level features (like edges and textures), and retraining the later layers to specialize in the new task.

Steps for configuring the model include:

1. **Load the Pre-trained Model**: Begin by loading the model architecture and weights, typically available through libraries like TensorFlow or PyTorch.
2. **Freeze the Early Layers**: Lock the parameters of the earlier layers, allowing them to retain their general feature-detecting capabilities. This is done by setting trainable=False for these layers.
3. **Modify the Output Layer**: Replace the output layer with a new layer(s) corresponding to the number of classes in your custom dataset. For example, if you're adapting an image classifier from ImageNet's 1,000 classes to classify 5 specific objects, replace the final dense layer with a new layer with 5 outputs.
4. **Add Custom Layers (Optional)**: To enhance the model's performance on your specific task, you can add additional layers to the network. Often, adding a fully connected layer before the output layer helps in

fine-tuning the model's adaptability to the new task.

3. Training (Fine-Tuning) the Model on Custom Data

Once the model is set up, the next step is to train it on your specific dataset. Fine-tuning generally involves the following steps:

1. **Compile the Model**: Choose an optimizer (like Adam or SGD), a loss function, and evaluation metrics suitable for your task. For example, use categorical cross-entropy for multi-class classification.
2. **Prepare the Data**: Organize and preprocess the data to match the input requirements of the model. Use data augmentation techniques like rotation, flipping, and scaling to increase the variety of input images, helping to prevent overfitting.
3. **Train the Model**: Begin training with a low learning rate, which helps maintain the pre-trained features in the frozen layers while allowing the unfrozen layers to learn the new task. Fine-tuning typically requires fewer epochs than training from scratch.
4. **Monitor Model Performance**: Track metrics such as accuracy and loss during training. Consider implementing early stopping, which halts training if the model's performance on a validation set stops improving, thus avoiding overfitting.

Practical Examples: Fine-Tuning VGG, ResNet, and Inception
Example 1: Fine-Tuning VGG for Plant Species Classification

Imagine you are building a classifier to identify plant species from leaf images. With VGG, you could leverage the model's capacity to learn intricate spatial hierarchies. Here's a high-level workflow:

- **Load the VGG model** with weights pre-trained on ImageNet.
- **Freeze the convolutional layers** and replace the final fully connected layers to output the correct number of plant species.
- **Augment the leaf images** (e.g., by rotating and scaling them) to enhance generalization.

- **Train the model** with a low learning rate on your plant dataset, focusing on fine-tuning the newly added layers for optimal species differentiation.

Example 2: Fine-Tuning ResNet for Medical Imaging Analysis

For a task like detecting tumors in MRI scans, ResNet's deep architecture and residual layers are advantageous due to the complexity of medical images. Here's how to approach this:

- **Load a pre-trained ResNet model** (e.g., ResNet-50) and lock the early residual layers.
- **Replace the output layer** to match the binary classification (e.g., "tumor" vs. "no tumor") needed for the medical task.
- **Utilize data augmentation techniques** (like varying brightness or adding noise) that mimic natural image variations in MRIs.
- **Train the model** carefully, observing model performance on validation data to ensure it generalizes well without overfitting.

Example 3: Fine-Tuning Inception for Satellite Image Classification

Inception's multi-scale feature extraction is ideal for complex tasks like classifying land types (forest, water, urban) in satellite imagery:

- **Load the Inception model** and freeze the initial layers, which capture multi-scale spatial features.
- **Replace the final layer** with a dense layer specific to your classes (e.g., forest, water, urban).
- **Use extensive data augmentation** (e.g., zoom, shear, and rotate) to mimic the variability in satellite imagery.
- **Train with a low learning rate**, focusing on updating only the final layers, and gradually increase the learning rate if deeper fine-tuning is needed.

Tips for Effective Fine-Tuning

1. **Start with a Low Learning Rate**: Use a smaller learning rate than you would for training from scratch, especially when fine-tuning the final layers. This approach avoids large weight updates that could disrupt the pre-trained features.

2. **Gradual Unfreezing**: If the model's performance plateaus, consider gradually unfreezing more layers, allowing the model to fine-tune deeper features related to the new task.

3. **Monitor for Overfitting**: With a smaller dataset, there's a high risk of overfitting. Use validation data and regularization techniques like dropout to ensure generalizability.

4. **Experiment with Different Models**: If the chosen pre-trained model doesn't yield satisfactory results, try a different architecture. Some tasks respond better to certain models based on their depth, structure, and feature extraction capabilities.

5. **Data Augmentation**: Augmenting your dataset not only improves model generalization but also helps the model learn features more robustly, especially if the training data is limited.

Fine-tuning pre-trained models like VGG, ResNet, and Inception allows you to leverage state-of-the-art architectures for custom tasks, providing a substantial boost in accuracy and efficiency compared to training from scratch. Each of these models brings unique strengths that can be matched to specific tasks based on the data characteristics and complexity of the problem. By carefully setting up, training, and validating your adapted model, you can achieve powerful results with minimal data and computational resources.

Generative Adversarial Networks (GANs): Introduction, Applications, and Building a Simple GAN

Generative Adversarial Networks, or GANs, are a groundbreaking architecture in deep learning that enable machines to generate data that closely resembles real-world examples. Introduced by Ian Goodfellow and his team in 2014, GANs use a unique framework of two competing networks—a generator and a discriminator—to produce high-quality, realistic outputs across a range of applications, from image generation to creating synthetic data. Their capacity to "imagine" new data has made GANs instrumental in fields like computer vision, creative content generation, and even scientific research.

This section provides an in-depth understanding of GANs, their key applications, and a practical guide to building a simple GAN for beginners. We'll cover their architecture, the training dynamics between the generator and discriminator, and how these networks work together to achieve remarkable results.

1. Introduction to Generative Adversarial Networks (GANs)

GANs consist of two neural networks—a generator and a discriminator—that engage in a game-like training process. Here's a breakdown of each component's role:

- **Generator**: The generator's task is to produce synthetic data that resembles real data as closely as possible. Starting from random noise, it learns to generate outputs that "fool" the discriminator.
- **Discriminator**: The discriminator's role is to differentiate between real data (from the dataset) and fake data (produced by the generator). By identifying fake samples, it pushes the generator to improve.

The training process involves these two networks in a zero-sum game, where the generator improves to create more realistic data, and the discriminator evolves to better distinguish real from fake data. This adversarial training framework leads both networks to higher performance, enabling the generation of data that can closely mimic real-world examples.

2. Applications of GANs

The versatility of GANs has made them indispensable in several domains, from creative fields to scientific research. Here are some popular applications of GANs, along with brief case studies:

- **Image Generation and Enhancement**: GANs are used to generate high-quality images from random noise, a process applied in creating synthetic images for data augmentation. They're also used in **super-resolution**, where GANs upscale low-resolution images to improve their clarity and detail.
- *Case Study*: A GAN-based super-resolution model was trained on satellite images to enhance resolution, allowing researchers to extract detailed information from low-quality satellite images for environmental monitoring.
- **Style Transfer and Artistic Generation**: GANs enable style transfer, allowing an image to adopt the style of another (e.g., making a photo look like a painting). In creative industries, GANs are leveraged to generate artistic content in new, unique styles.
- *Case Study*: In an AI-driven art project, a GAN was trained to produce artwork inspired by the works of famous painters. The result was unique, original digital art that blended traditional techniques with AI's imaginative capabilities.
- **Data Augmentation**: GANs are increasingly used to generate synthetic data for training machine learning models, especially in domains where real data is scarce or difficult to obtain (e.g., medical imaging).
- *Case Study*: In medical imaging, GANs generated realistic X-ray images to augment limited datasets, improving the robustness and accuracy of models trained on medical diagnostics.
- **Text-to-Image Generation**: GANs can translate textual descriptions into images, creating visual representations of abstract concepts. This has implications for fields like advertising, where visual content is generated directly from written descriptions.
- *Case Study*: In e-commerce, GANs were applied to generate product images based on textual descriptions, allowing retailers to showcase new products in an automated manner without needing actual photographs.
- **Video Generation and Prediction**: GANs are used to generate realistic video frames and predict future frames based on previous sequences, which is valuable in applications such as video compression

and autonomous vehicle technology.

- *Case Study*: GANs trained on driving footage are used to predict the next few frames, assisting self-driving cars in understanding potential future scenarios and making safer decisions.

3. Building a Simple GAN: Step-by-Step Guide

Building a GAN involves creating and training both the generator and discriminator models. In this guide, we'll build a basic GAN designed to generate handwritten digits similar to those in the MNIST dataset.

Step 1: Set Up the Generator and Discriminator

Generator Architecture: The generator starts with a vector of random noise as input, which it transforms through a series of dense and convolutional layers to produce an image that resembles those in the MNIST dataset.

- The input to the generator is typically a random noise vector, allowing it to explore a variety of output possibilities.
- The generator's output layer uses a tanh activation function, yielding values between -1 and 1, which corresponds to the normalized range of image pixel values.

Discriminator Architecture: The discriminator is a binary classifier that outputs the probability of whether an input image is real or generated.

- It takes an image as input and processes it through convolutional layers.
- The final layer uses a sigmoid activation function to provide a probability score indicating the likelihood that the image is real.

Step 2: Implement the Adversarial Training Process

1. **Compile the Discriminator**: Use a binary cross-entropy loss function, which is suitable for binary classification tasks. Set the discrimi-

nator's weights to be trainable.

2. **Combine the Models**: Create a combined GAN model that stacks the generator and discriminator. Importantly, while training the combined model, set the discriminator's weights to non-trainable, ensuring only the generator is updated based on the adversarial loss.

3. **Define the Training Loop**:

- Generate a batch of random noise vectors and pass them through the generator to produce synthetic images.
- Sample a batch of real images from the dataset and combine them with the generated images.
- Train the discriminator on this combined set, adjusting its weights to improve its ability to distinguish real from fake images.
- Train the generator through the combined model, adjusting its weights to produce images that increasingly fool the discriminator.

Repeat the Training Steps: Iterate this process over many epochs, refining the generator and discriminator iteratively. The generator becomes better at creating realistic images, while the discriminator gets better at distinguishing them.

Step 3: Evaluate the GAN's Performance

As training progresses, monitor the quality of generated images by visually inspecting samples or calculating metrics such as the Inception Score or Frechet Inception Distance, which measure the realism and variety of generated samples.

Practical Code for Building a Simple GAN

Here's a minimal code outline for implementing a GAN in Python using TensorFlow and Keras:

```
python
```

```python
import tensorflow as tf
from tensorflow.keras import layers

# Generator model
def build_generator(noise_dim):
    model = tf.keras.Sequential([
        layers.Dense(128, activation='relu',
        input_shape=(noise_dim,)),
        layers.Dense(256, activation='relu'),
        layers.Dense(784, activation='tanh')  # Output size for
        28x28 image
    ])
    return model

# Discriminator model
def build_discriminator():
    model = tf.keras.Sequential([
        layers.Dense(256, activation='relu', input_shape=(784,)),
        layers.Dense(128, activation='relu'),
        layers.Dense(1, activation='sigmoid')  # Output
        probability
    ])
    return model

# Instantiate models
noise_dim = 100
generator = build_generator(noise_dim)
discriminator = build_discriminator()

# Compile discriminator
discriminator.compile(optimizer='adam',
loss='binary_crossentropy', metrics=['accuracy'])

# Combined GAN model
discriminator.trainable = False
gan_input = layers.Input(shape=(noise_dim,))
generated_image = generator(gan_input)
gan_output = discriminator(generated_image)
gan = tf.keras.Model(gan_input, gan_output)
gan.compile(optimizer='adam', loss='binary_crossentropy')
```

```
# Training loop (simplified)
import numpy as np
real_data = np.random.normal(size=(1000, 784))  # Placeholder for
real images
batch_size = 32
for epoch in range(epochs):
    # Generate fake images
    noise = np.random.normal(size=(batch_size, noise_dim))
    fake_images = generator.predict(noise)

    # Train discriminator
    real_labels = np.ones((batch_size, 1))
    fake_labels = np.zeros((batch_size, 1))
    discriminator.train_on_batch(real_data[:batch_size],
    real_labels)
    discriminator.train_on_batch(fake_images, fake_labels)

    # Train generator (via GAN model)
    misleading_labels = np.ones((batch_size, 1))
    gan.train_on_batch(noise, misleading_labels)
```

GANs represent a powerful class of models for generating realistic data across various domains. By engaging in adversarial training, the generator and discriminator refine each other's performance, enabling GANs to produce outputs that often rival real-world data in quality.

Hands-On: Creating Images with GANs – A Practical Guide

Creating images with GANs is an exciting application that lets us produce realistic, synthetic images by leveraging the generator-discriminator dynamic. In this guide, we'll walk through a step-by-step process for generating images, covering the necessary components and practical considerations. By the end, you'll have a functional GAN capable of producing images similar to those in a target dataset.

We'll use TensorFlow and Keras for this guide, as these libraries simplify building, training, and optimizing GANs.

Step 1: Import Libraries and Load Dataset

Start by importing the necessary libraries and loading a dataset. Here, we'll use the MNIST dataset, which contains 28x28 grayscale images of handwritten digits, as a starting point for image generation. MNIST is ideal for beginners due to its simplicity and accessibility.

python

```
import tensorflow as tf
from tensorflow.keras import layers
import numpy as np
import matplotlib.pyplot as plt

# Load the MNIST dataset
(train_images, _), (_, _) = tf.keras.datasets.mnist.load_data()
train_images = (train_images - 127.5) / 127.5  # Normalize to
range [-1, 1]
train_images = train_images.reshape(train_images.shape[0], 784)
# Flatten images
batch_size = 256
noise_dim = 100
```

Step 2: Build the Generator

The generator starts with random noise and transforms it into a 28x28 image. For simplicity, we'll use a dense network to output flat 784-dimensional vectors (one for each pixel in a 28x28 image). More complex GANs use convolutional layers, but dense layers work well for a basic example.

python

```
def build_generator(noise_dim):
    model = tf.keras.Sequential([
```

```python
        layers.Dense(256, activation='relu',
        input_shape=(noise_dim,)),
        layers.Dense(512, activation='relu'),
        layers.Dense(1024, activation='relu'),
        layers.Dense(784, activation='tanh')  # Output size
        matches image dimensions
    ])
    return model

generator = build_generator(noise_dim)
```

Step 3: Build the Discriminator

The discriminator's role is to determine if an image is real or generated. It takes a 784-dimensional image as input and outputs a single probability value indicating its likelihood of authenticity.

python

```python
def build_discriminator():
    model = tf.keras.Sequential([
        layers.Dense(1024, activation='relu', input_shape=(784,)),
        layers.Dense(512, activation='relu'),
        layers.Dense(256, activation='relu'),
        layers.Dense(1, activation='sigmoid')  # Binary
        classification output
    ])
    return model

discriminator = build_discriminator()
discriminator.compile(optimizer='adam',
loss='binary_crossentropy', metrics=['accuracy'])
```

Step 4: Create the GAN Model

Now, we'll stack the generator and discriminator to form the full GAN model. Importantly, we set the discriminator to be non-trainable while training the generator to ensure only the generator's weights are updated based on the GAN's loss.

```python
python
```

```python
def build_gan(generator, discriminator):
    discriminator.trainable = False
    model = tf.keras.Sequential([generator, discriminator])
    model.compile(optimizer='adam', loss='binary_crossentropy')
    return model

gan = build_gan(generator, discriminator)
```

Step 5: Define the Training Function

Training a GAN involves iterating over a series of steps. We'll generate fake images with the generator, train the discriminator on both real and fake images, and then update the generator to improve its ability to "fool" the discriminator. This adversarial training process gradually enhances the quality of generated images.

1. **Generate Fake Images**: Start with random noise vectors and use the generator to create fake images.
2. **Train the Discriminator**: Train the discriminator on both real images (from the dataset) and fake images (from the generator).
3. **Train the Generator**: Train the generator through the GAN model by updating it to create images that can better fool the discriminator.

```python
python
```

```python
def train_gan(gan, generator, discriminator, dataset, noise_dim,
epochs=50, batch_size=256):
    for epoch in range(epochs):
        for _ in range(len(dataset) // batch_size):
            # Prepare real and fake images
            real_images = dataset[np.random.randint(0,
            dataset.shape[0], batch_size)]
```

```
        noise = np.random.normal(0, 1, (batch_size,
        noise_dim))
        fake_images = generator.predict(noise)

        # Labels for training
        real_labels = np.ones((batch_size, 1))
        fake_labels = np.zeros((batch_size, 1))

        # Train discriminator
        d_loss_real =
        discriminator.train_on_batch(real_images, real_labels)
        d_loss_fake =
        discriminator.train_on_batch(fake_images, fake_labels)

        # Train generator through the GAN model
        misleading_labels = np.ones((batch_size, 1))  # Train
        generator to "fool" discriminator
        g_loss = gan.train_on_batch(noise, misleading_labels)

    # Log progress
    print(f"Epoch {epoch + 1}/{epochs}, D Loss Real:
    {d_loss_real}, D Loss Fake: {d_loss_fake}, G Loss:
    {g_loss}")

    # Generate images at the end of each epoch
    generate_and_save_images(generator, epoch + 1, noise_dim)

def generate_and_save_images(generator, epoch, noise_dim,
examples=16):
    noise = np.random.normal(0, 1, (examples, noise_dim))
    generated_images = generator.predict(noise).reshape(examples,
    28, 28)
    fig, axes = plt.subplots(4, 4, figsize=(4, 4))
    for i, ax in enumerate(axes.flat):
        ax.imshow(generated_images[i], cmap='gray')
        ax.axis('off')
    plt.show()
```

Step 6: Train and Evaluate the GAN

With all components in place, you can start training your GAN model.

Each epoch will refine the quality of generated images as the generator learns from feedback provided by the discriminator.

python

```
# Preprocess dataset and start training
train_images = train_images.astype('float32')
train_gan(gan, generator, discriminator, train_images, noise_dim,
epochs=50, batch_size=batch_size)
```

During training, the GAN alternates between refining the generator and discriminator. This process gradually improves the generator's ability to produce realistic images, while the discriminator becomes more accurate at distinguishing between real and fake images.

Observing Results: Visualize Generated Images

Each epoch produces an updated set of images. As training progresses, you should observe that generated images evolve from random noise into more coherent and structured images that resemble those in the dataset. You can adjust parameters like the number of epochs or the architecture of the generator and discriminator to fine-tune results.

GANs offer a unique way of synthesizing realistic data, and their applications are extensive. With this practical understanding of GANs and the hands-on exercise completed, you're now equipped to experiment with more advanced architectures and explore GAN-based projects, such as super-resolution, style transfer, and text-to-image synthesis.

Transformers and Attention Mechanisms: Basics of the Transformer Model and Applications in NLP

Transformers have revolutionized deep learning, especially in natural language processing (NLP), by enabling more efficient and accurate handling of sequential data. At the core of the Transformer model is the attention mechanism, which allows it to focus on relevant parts of input sequences. This section provides a foundational understanding of how Transformers work, their main components, and how they apply to various NLP tasks.

Understanding the Need for Transformers

Traditional neural network architectures, such as recurrent neural networks (RNNs) and long short-term memory networks (LSTMs), process data sequentially, making them prone to limitations in handling long sequences or retaining context over extended inputs. The Transformer model, introduced by Vaswani et al. in the 2017 paper "Attention is All You Need," overcomes these limitations by using self-attention mechanisms to process all input tokens simultaneously, allowing it to model long-range dependencies more effectively.

Key Components of the Transformer Model

The Transformer architecture consists of an encoder-decoder structure, each with multiple layers composed of several important components:

1. **Self-Attention Mechanism**: This mechanism allows the model to weigh the importance of different words in a sentence relative to each other. Each word in the input is given an "attention score" with respect to every other word, enabling the model to capture context and relationships without processing the sequence strictly from left to right.

2. **Positional Encoding**: Since Transformers do not process data sequentially, positional encoding is added to input tokens to help the model understand the order of the sequence. This encoding provides each token with a unique position in the sentence, which becomes essential for tasks where word order is meaningful.

3. **Multi-Head Attention**: This extends the self-attention mechanism by creating multiple "heads" that focus on different parts of the sequence, allowing the model to capture various aspects of context within a single layer. Each head performs self-attention independently and is then concatenated and linearly transformed, providing a more nuanced understanding of the data.

4. **Feed-Forward Neural Networks**: Each encoder and decoder layer

includes a feed-forward neural network that applies nonlinear transformations to the attention output, further refining it before passing it
to the next layer.

5. **Layer Normalization and Residual Connections**: These components help stabilize training by normalizing the output of each layer and
adding the original input back to the output after each layer (residual
connections), which helps maintain information flow throughout the
network.

The Encoder and Decoder Stack

1. **Encoder**: The encoder processes the input sequence to create a
continuous representation that captures the contextual information
of each token. Each layer in the encoder consists of a self-attention
mechanism and a feed-forward network.

2. **Decoder**: The decoder generates output sequences based on the
encoded representation from the encoder. It uses two attention
mechanisms: one for the encoder output (to extract contextual
information) and one for the partially generated output sequence (to
ensure each token in the output attends to the relevant input tokens).

In practice, many Transformer-based models used for NLP tasks, such as
BERT and GPT, only use the encoder or decoder component (not both),
depending on the application.

The Attention Mechanism: How it Works

Attention calculates the relevance of one word to another within the input.
The process can be summarized as follows:

1. **Query, Key, and Value Vectors**: For each input token, three vectors—
query (Q), key (K), and value (V)—are created. These vectors help
calculate the importance of each token relative to every other token.

2. **Calculating Attention Scores**: The attention score between two

tokens is calculated by taking the dot product of the query and key vectors, scaled and normalized. This produces weights that represent the "focus" the model should have on each word.

3. **Weighted Sum**: Each word's value vector is multiplied by the attention weights and then summed up to create the final representation for each token in the context of the sentence.

Mathematically, this process can be expressed as:

$$\text{Attention}(Q, K, V) = \text{softmax}\left(\frac{Q \cdot K^T}{\sqrt{d_k}}\right) V$$

where d_k is the dimensionality of the key vectors, and the softmax function ensures that the attention scores are normalized.

Advantages of Transformers

- **Parallelization**: Unlike RNNs, Transformers process all tokens in a sequence simultaneously, allowing them to leverage GPU/TPU hardware for faster computation.
- **Better Handling of Long-Range Dependencies**: With self-attention, Transformers can capture relationships between distant tokens effectively.
- **Scalability**: Transformers can scale to very large models and datasets, which has led to significant breakthroughs in language modeling and generation.

Applications of Transformers in NLP

Transformers have become the backbone of state-of-the-art NLP models. Here are some prominent applications:

1. **Language Translation**: Models like Google's T5 and Facebook's M2M-100 use Transformers to translate text between languages, significantly improving translation quality by handling complex language structures and idiomatic expressions.

2. **Sentiment Analysis**: BERT and other Transformer-based models perform sentiment analysis by evaluating the emotional tone in text. They are widely used for tasks like customer feedback analysis, brand sentiment monitoring, and social media sentiment tracking.

3. **Question Answering**: Transformers are particularly effective for question-answering systems, enabling models like BERT and RoBERTa to extract answers to questions from large textual corpora with high accuracy.

4. **Text Generation**: GPT (Generative Pre-trained Transformer) models, such as GPT-3, excel in generating human-like text for various applications, including conversational agents, story writing, and code generation.

5. **Text Summarization**: Transformers can condense lengthy articles, documents, or conversations into concise summaries. Models like BART and T5 are optimized for this task, generating coherent and contextually accurate summaries.

6. **Named Entity Recognition (NER)**: Identifying and classifying entities like names, dates, and locations in text is another area where Transformers excel. These models are essential for building information extraction systems used in research, legal tech, and medical record analysis.

7. **Speech Recognition**: While primarily based on RNNs historically, recent advancements have seen the adoption of Transformer-based models for transcribing spoken language with high accuracy, especially in applications like voice assistants.

Transformer-Based NLP Models

1. **BERT (Bidirectional Encoder Representations from Transform-**

ers): BERT leverages bidirectional training on vast amounts of text to provide deep contextual understanding. It is designed for tasks that require full sentence understanding and is widely used in NLU (Natural Language Understanding) applications.

2. **GPT (Generative Pre-trained Transformer)**: GPT models, such as GPT-2 and GPT-3, are autoregressive models trained to predict the next word in a sequence, making them powerful for text generation tasks.

3. **T5 (Text-to-Text Transfer Transformer)**: T5 reformulates NLP problems as text-to-text tasks, where both input and output are in natural language. This versatility allows it to perform various tasks, from translation to summarization, within a unified framework.

4. **RoBERTa (Robustly Optimized BERT)**: RoBERTa is a variation of BERT that modifies training techniques for enhanced performance, excelling in tasks like question answering and text classification.

Transformers and attention mechanisms are foundational to modern NLP, with applications ranging from simple text classification to complex conversational AI systems. Their flexibility and effectiveness in handling sequential data have cemented Transformers as essential components of advanced NLP systems, making them a critical tool for any deep learning practitioner focused on language and sequence modeling.

Training, Tuning, and Optimizing Models

H yperparameter Tuning: Grid Search, Random Search, and Best Practices
Hyperparameter tuning is one of the most crucial steps in building a deep learning model that performs well on unseen data. While machine learning algorithms have certain parameters that are learned from the data (e.g., weights and biases), hyperparameters are settings that must be manually specified before training. These parameters control the learning process itself and have a significant impact on the model's performance.

In this section, we'll explore common techniques for hyperparameter tuning, including **Grid Search**, **Random Search**, and discuss best practices to help you efficiently fine-tune your models for optimal results.

What Are Hyperparameters?

Before diving into hyperparameter tuning techniques, it is essential to understand what hyperparameters are. They are parameters that control the behavior of the model during training and are set manually before the learning process begins. Examples of hyperparameters in deep learning include:

- **Learning Rate**: The step size used in updating the model's weights during training. A higher learning rate can lead to faster convergence but risks overshooting the optimal point, while a lower rate might result in slower convergence or getting stuck in local minima.

- **Number of Epochs**: The number of times the model will iterate over the entire training dataset.
- **Batch Size**: The number of training examples utilized in one iteration of model training.
- **Number of Hidden Layers and Neurons**: The architecture of the model, which includes the depth (number of layers) and width (number of neurons per layer).
- **Dropout Rate**: A regularization technique used to prevent overfitting by randomly dropping units during training.
- **Optimizer**: The algorithm used to minimize the loss function (e.g., Adam, SGD).

Fine-tuning these hyperparameters can make a substantial difference in model accuracy, generalization ability, and training efficiency.

Hyperparameter Tuning Methods

The process of selecting the best set of hyperparameters is called **hyperparameter optimization**. Several methods exist to help automate this process and improve model performance. The two most popular techniques for hyperparameter tuning are **Grid Search** and **Random Search**.

Grid Search: Exhaustive Search Over Hyperparameter Space

Grid Search is one of the most straightforward methods for hyperparameter tuning. It involves defining a grid of hyperparameters and evaluating the model performance for every possible combination of the hyperparameters. For example, if you want to tune the learning rate and batch size, you might define a grid like this:

- Learning Rate: [0.001, 0.01, 0.1]
- Batch Size: [16, 32, 64]

Grid Search will then train the model for every combination of these values (in this case, 9 different combinations) and evaluate its performance using cross-validation or a validation set.

Advantages:

- **Exhaustive Search**: Grid search ensures that all possible combinations of hyperparameters are tested, potentially leading to the best combination for the model.
- **Simple to Implement**: It is conceptually easy to understand and implement in most machine learning frameworks, such as scikit-learn, TensorFlow, and Keras.

Disadvantages:

- **Computationally Expensive**: Grid search can be very time-consuming when you have a large hyperparameter space or computationally expensive models, as it exhaustively searches all possible combinations.
- **Inefficiency**: Grid search can lead to inefficiency since it tests combinations that might not be necessary. For example, the best learning rate for a particular batch size might not need to be tested against all the other batch sizes.

Use Case: Grid search is effective when you have a small set of hyperparameters to tune, and you can afford to test all combinations exhaustively. It is often used in initial experiments when searching for a reasonable hyperparameter range.

Random Search: Sampling Hyperparameters Randomly

Random Search, unlike Grid Search, does not evaluate all possible combinations of hyperparameters. Instead, it randomly samples values from predefined ranges or distributions for each hyperparameter and evaluates the model based on those choices.

For example, instead of exhaustively testing every combination of the learning rate and batch size, Random Search might randomly sample a learning rate of 0.01 with a batch size of 32, then 0.001 with 64, and so on, until it reaches the desired number of evaluations.

Advantages:

- **Efficient for Large Spaces**: Random search is more efficient than grid search for large hyperparameter spaces because it does not waste resources on testing combinations that are unlikely to work well.
- **Exploration of the Hyperparameter Space**: By sampling randomly, it is more likely to explore different regions of the hyperparameter space, potentially finding the optimal configuration faster.

Disadvantages:

- **No Guarantee of Exhaustiveness**: Unlike Grid Search, Random Search does not guarantee that it will explore the entire hyperparameter space, which might lead to suboptimal performance if the hyperparameters are not sampled effectively.
- **Risk of Missing Optimal Hyperparameters**: If the number of iterations is too small or the search space is too wide, random search may miss the optimal values for the hyperparameters.

Use Case: Random search is often preferred when the search space is large, and computational resources are limited. It can also be more useful when exploring complex models where fine-tuning all hyperparameters exhaustively might not be practical.

Best Practices for Hyperparameter Tuning

Both Grid Search and Random Search are useful tools for hyperparameter tuning, but understanding the best practices can further optimize the tuning process, saving time and resources while improving model performance.

1. **Start with a Broad Search**: Initially, perform a random search over a broad range of hyperparameters. This will give you a better idea of which parameters affect performance the most and which values are worth fine-tuning more precisely.
2. **Use a Validation Set or Cross-Validation**: To evaluate the perfor-

mance of each hyperparameter combination, use a separate validation set (or cross-validation) to avoid overfitting the model to the training data. This gives a better estimate of how the model will perform on unseen data.

3. **Focus on Key Hyperparameters**: While it is tempting to tune all hyperparameters, some may have a more significant impact on model performance than others. Start by tuning the most influential parameters (such as learning rate, number of layers, and batch size), and then refine less critical ones.

4. **Use Early Stopping**: Hyperparameter tuning can be time-consuming, so it's important to use techniques like early stopping to halt the training process if the model's performance on the validation set stops improving. This prevents wasting computational resources on unpromising hyperparameter combinations.

5. **Keep Track of Results**: Use systematic logging and tracking for each hyperparameter combination and its performance. Tools like **TensorBoard** and **MLflow** allow you to track hyperparameters and results, making it easier to identify which configurations lead to the best results.

6. **Use Automated Hyperparameter Optimization**: Automated hyperparameter optimization techniques like **Bayesian Optimization**, **Hyperband**, or **Genetic Algorithms** can be more efficient than Grid Search and Random Search. These methods use advanced techniques to intelligently select hyperparameters based on previous trials, aiming to converge faster to optimal values.

7. **Consider Computational Resources**: Always consider the computational cost of hyperparameter tuning. If you're working with large datasets or deep networks, the time it takes to perform hyperparameter optimization can become prohibitively expensive. Use parallelization and distributed computing where possible to speed up the process.

Hyperparameter tuning is a critical aspect of deep learning that can significantly influence the performance of a model. While **Grid Search** and **Random Search** are popular methods, they each have their pros and cons. Grid Search is exhaustive but computationally expensive, while Random Search is more efficient and can explore a larger space in a shorter time. Adopting best practices, such as focusing on key hyperparameters, using cross-validation, and leveraging automated optimization tools, can make the tuning process much more efficient.

In the next chapter, we will explore advanced optimization techniques, such as learning rate schedules, advanced regularization methods, and methods for avoiding overfitting, to ensure that your models not only perform well on training data but also generalize effectively to unseen data.

Regularization Techniques: Dropout, L2 Regularization, and Batch Normalization

In deep learning, **regularization** refers to techniques used to prevent overfitting, which occurs when a model learns to perform exceptionally well on training data but fails to generalize to new, unseen data. Overfitting is a significant issue in deep learning due to the vast number of parameters models can have, especially in large, complex architectures. Regularization methods help keep the model from becoming too tailored to the training data and improve its ability to generalize.

In this section, we will discuss three important regularization techniques used in deep learning: **Dropout, L2 Regularization**, and **Batch Normalization**. Each of these methods plays a vital role in improving the robustness and performance of models, particularly when dealing with large datasets and deep architectures.

Dropout: Randomly Disabling Neurons to Prevent Overfitting

Dropout is one of the most widely used regularization techniques in deep learning. The basic idea behind dropout is to randomly "drop" or deactivate a certain fraction of the neurons in the network during training. This prevents the model from relying too heavily on any one neuron and forces it to learn more robust features. During each training iteration, a random set of neurons is selected and temporarily removed from the network, meaning that they do not participate in both forward propagation and backpropagation. However, at test time, all neurons are used, but their output is scaled down according to the dropout rate.

How Dropout Works:

- During training, for each mini-batch, neurons are randomly selected (typically by a Bernoulli distribution) and set to zero with a probability of ppp, where ppp is the dropout rate.
- For example, if you have a dropout rate of 0.5 (50%), then approximately half of the neurons in the layer will be randomly disabled for each training iteration.
- The key to dropout's success is that it forces the network to learn a more distributed, robust representation of the data rather than relying too heavily on specific neurons or parts of the model.

Advantages:

- **Prevents Overfitting**: By preventing any one neuron from becoming overly important, dropout encourages the network to generalize better and reduces overfitting.
- **Improves Model Robustness**: Since different subsets of neurons are used at each training iteration, the model learns to make predictions based on a variety of combinations of features, making it more resilient to new data.

Disadvantages:

- **Slower Convergence**: Dropout can slow down training because it effectively reduces the number of neurons available during training, which can increase the number of epochs needed to converge.
- **Can Underfit**: If the dropout rate is too high, the network might not be

able to learn enough from the data, leading to underfitting. Therefore, it is essential to experiment with the dropout rate to find the optimal value.

Common Use Cases:

- Dropout is most commonly applied to the fully connected layers in deep neural networks, including convolutional neural networks (CNNs) and fully connected networks.
- Dropout rates of 0.2 to 0.5 are typical, but this can vary based on the complexity of the task and dataset.

L2 Regularization: Penalizing Large Weights to Encourage Simpler Models

L2 Regularization, also known as **weight decay**, is another regularization technique that works by adding a penalty term to the loss function, discouraging large weights in the model. The key idea behind L2 regularization is that large weights indicate a model that is overfitting the training data, as it can memorize specific patterns. By adding a penalty proportional to the square of the magnitude of the weights, L2 regularization encourages the model to keep the weights smaller and, thus, less likely to overfit.

How L2 Regularization Works:

- In L2 regularization, the original loss function (e.g., mean squared error or cross-entropy) is augmented by adding the sum of the squares of the weights multiplied by a regularization factor $\lambda\lambda$.
- The modified loss function becomes:

$$L(\theta) = L_{original} + \lambda \sum_{i=1}^{n} \theta_i^2$$

where:

- $L_{original}$ is the original loss function,
- λ is the regularization coefficient that controls the strength of the penalty, and
- θ_i are the model's weights.

- The factor λ controls how much penalty is added. A larger λ encourages smaller weights and a simpler model, while a smaller λ allows for more complex models. The value of λ should be chosen carefully through cross-validation or other optimization methods.

Advantages:

- **Prevents Overfitting**: By penalizing large weights, L2 regularization prevents the model from becoming too complex and overfitting to the training data.
- **Improves Model Generalization**: Models that are penalized for large weights tend to generalize better and are less likely to memorize specific noise patterns in the data.

Disadvantages:

- **May Slow Convergence**: Similar to dropout, L2 regularization can slow down training since the model has to find a balance between minimizing the original loss and the regularization term.
- **Does Not Eliminate Weights**: Unlike L1 regularization, which can force weights to be exactly zero (leading to sparsity), L2 regularization only reduces their size. As a result, it may not result in feature selection.

Common Use Cases:

- L2 regularization is commonly used in almost all types of neural networks, including CNNs, RNNs, and feedforward networks.
- It is often used alongside other techniques such as dropout to further improve generalization.

Batch Normalization: Accelerating Training and Reducing Overfitting

Batch Normalization (BN) is another effective technique for regulariz-
ing deep neural networks. Introduced by Sergey Ioffe and Christian Szegedy
in 2015, batch normalization normalizes the inputs of each layer so that
they have a mean of zero and a variance of one. This helps to stabilize
the learning process by reducing the internal covariate shift, which is the
change in the distribution of layer inputs during training. By normalizing
activations, batch normalization allows for faster convergence and more
stable training, often allowing for higher learning rates.

How Batch Normalization Works:

- For each mini-batch during training, batch normalization computes
  the mean and variance of the activations for each feature.
- The activations are then normalized by subtracting the mean and
  dividing by the standard deviation.

$$\hat{x} = \frac{x - \mu}{\sigma}$$

where:

- μ is the mean of the batch,
- σ is the standard deviation of the batch, and
- x is the input to the layer.

- After normalizing the data, batch normalization applies two additional
  learnable parameters: a scaling factor γ\gamma$\gamma$ and a shifting factor
  β\beta$\beta$. These parameters allow the model to adjust the normalized
  values to ensure they can represent the data well.

$$y = \gamma \hat{x} + \beta$$

Advantages:

- **Faster Convergence**: Batch normalization reduces the internal covariate shift and allows for faster convergence during training. This can lead to faster training times and improved model performance.
- **Prevents Overfitting**: By adding a small amount of noise to the model (due to the mini-batch computations), batch normalization acts as a form of regularization, helping to prevent overfitting.
- **Increased Learning Rate**: With batch normalization, higher learning rates can be used without the risk of diverging, leading to more efficient training.

Disadvantages:

- **Increased Computation**: Batch normalization adds additional computation overhead to the training process since it requires calculating the mean and variance for each mini-batch.
- **Sensitive to Batch Size**: The effectiveness of batch normalization can be influenced by the batch size, and it may not work well for very small batches.

Common Use Cases:

- Batch normalization is widely used in deep neural networks, including CNNs, feedforward networks, and more. It is particularly useful when training very deep networks, as it helps to avoid vanishing or exploding gradients.
- It is often used in conjunction with other regularization techniques like dropout or L2 regularization.

Regularization is an essential part of training deep learning models, as it helps to prevent overfitting and ensures that the model generalizes well to new data. The techniques we discussed — **Dropout, L2 Regularization**, and **Batch Normalization** — each provide unique ways to regularize a model, with different strengths and trade-offs.

In practice, it is common to combine multiple regularization techniques, such as applying both dropout and L2 regularization, or using batch normalization along with other methods. The key to effective regularization is experimentation and tuning, as the right combination of techniques depends on the specific task, dataset, and model architecture.

As we continue, we'll explore other advanced optimization techniques, like learning rate schedules and early stopping, to fine-tune models and ensure they achieve optimal performance while minimizing overfitting.

Model Evaluation Metrics: Precision, Recall, F1 Score, and ROC-AUC

Evaluating the performance of deep learning models is crucial to understand how well they generalize and make predictions on new, unseen data. While traditional accuracy is a useful metric, it can sometimes be misleading, especially in the case of imbalanced datasets. To obtain a clearer picture of model performance, we turn to more advanced evaluation metrics such as **Precision, Recall, F1 Score**, and **ROC-AUC**. Each of these metrics provides a deeper insight into how well a model performs, particularly in classification tasks where the cost of false positives and false negatives may differ.

In this section, we will explore these important metrics, explain their meanings, and provide practical examples of when and how to use them.

Precision: The Proportion of True Positives Among Predicted Positives

Precision is a metric used to evaluate the accuracy of positive predictions made by a model. It is particularly important when the consequences of false positives (incorrectly predicting the positive class) are costly. For instance, in medical diagnosis, a false positive might lead to unnecessary tests or treatments.

Definition: Precision measures the proportion of correctly predicted positive instances (true positives) out of all instances that the model predicted as positive (true positives + false positives). Mathematically, it is expressed as:

$$\text{Precision} = \frac{\text{True Positives}}{\text{True Positives} + \text{False Positives}}$$

Interpretation:
- A **high precision** means that when the model predicts a positive outcome, it is likely to be correct.
- A **low precision** indicates that the model frequently predicts positives that turn out to be false.

Example: In a binary classification problem where the goal is to detect spam emails:

- True Positives (TP): Emails correctly identified as spam.
- False Positives (FP): Non-spam emails incorrectly identified as spam.

If the model predicts 100 emails as spam, and 90 of those are actually spam (TP), while 10 are not (FP), the precision is:

Precision=9090+10=0.9\text{Precision} = \frac{90}{90 + 10} = 0.9Precision=90+1090=0.9

This means 90% of the emails predicted as spam are actually spam, and the model is reliable in its positive predictions.

Recall: The Proportion of Actual Positives Correctly Identified

Recall, also known as **Sensitivity** or **True Positive Rate**, is a metric that focuses on the ability of a model to identify all positive instances in the data. Unlike precision, which is concerned with the accuracy of positive predictions, recall emphasizes finding all actual positives, even at the risk of some false positives. Recall is particularly useful when missing a positive instance (false negative) is costly, such as in disease detection where failing to identify a sick patient could have serious consequences.

Definition: Recall measures the proportion of true positives correctly identified by the model out of all actual positives (true positives + false negatives). It is given by:

$$\text{Recall} = \frac{\text{True Positives}}{\text{True Positives} + \text{False Negatives}}$$

Interpretation:

- A **high recall** means the model is good at identifying positive cases, with few false negatives.
- A **low recall** means the model is missing a significant number of actual positive cases, resulting in a higher number of false negatives.

Example: In the case of a medical test for detecting cancer:

- True Positives (TP): Patients correctly diagnosed as having cancer.
- False Negatives (FN): Patients incorrectly diagnosed as healthy (missed cancer cases).

If the model correctly identifies 90 out of 100 cancer patients (TP), but misses 10 (FN), the recall would be:

In this case, 90% of the actual cancer cases are correctly identified, which is critical when dealing with life-threatening conditions.

F1 Score: The Balance Between Precision and Recall

The **F1 Score** is a single metric that combines both precision and recall. It is the harmonic mean of precision and recall and provides a balanced measure of a model's performance when both false positives and false negatives are important. The F1 score is especially useful when you need to balance the trade-off between precision and recall, as it penalizes extreme values in either metric.

Definition: The F1 score is calculated as:

$$F1\ Score = 2 \cdot \frac{Precision \cdot Recall}{Precision + Recall}$$

Interpretation:

- The F1 score ranges from 0 to 1, where 1 is the best possible performance (perfect precision and recall) and 0 indicates the worst performance (either precision or recall is zero).
- A high F1 score means that the model has both high precision and high recall, providing a good balance between minimizing false positives and false negatives.

Example: If a model has a precision of 0.9 and a recall of 0.8, the F1 score would be:

$$F1\ Score = 2 \cdot \frac{0.9 \cdot 0.8}{0.9 + 0.8} = 0.84$$

This indicates that the model has a good balance between precision and recall, but there is still room for improvement in either metric.

ROC-AUC: Evaluating Model Performance Across Different Thresholds

ROC-AUC stands for **Receiver Operating Characteristic** and **Area Under the Curve**. It is a performance measurement for classification problems at various threshold settings. The ROC curve plots the True Positive Rate (Recall) against the False Positive Rate (FPR) for different classification thresholds. The **AUC** (Area Under the Curve) represents the model's ability to discriminate between positive and negative classes. A higher AUC indicates a better-performing model.

Definition:

- The **True Positive Rate (TPR)** is the same as recall, and the **False Positive Rate (FPR)** is calculated as:

$$FPR = \frac{\text{False Positives}}{\text{False Positives} + \text{True Negatives}}$$

- The **ROC curve** plots TPR on the y-axis and FPR on the x-axis.
- The **AUC** represents the area under the ROC curve and gives a summary of the model's performance across all possible classification thresholds.

Interpretation:

- An **AUC of 1.0** represents a perfect model, which can perfectly separate positive and negative cases.
- An **AUC of 0.5** represents a model that performs no better than random guessing.
- A higher AUC indicates a better ability of the model to distinguish between the positive and negative classes.

Example: For a binary classification problem, the ROC-AUC might range from 0 to 1, where:

- An AUC of 0.95 would indicate an excellent model that can reliably differentiate between classes.
- An AUC of 0.7 would indicate a model that is decent but not perfect.

Precision, recall, F1 score, and ROC-AUC are essential metrics for evaluating the performance of classification models, especially when dealing with imbalanced datasets or when the cost of false positives and false negatives is not equal. While precision and recall focus on different aspects of model performance, the F1 score combines both to provide a balanced measure. ROC-AUC, on the other hand, allows for evaluating model performance across various thresholds and is particularly useful for models with probabilistic outputs.

By understanding these metrics and applying them appropriately, you can get a much clearer picture of your model's strengths and weaknesses, and make informed decisions about how to improve its performance. As we continue, we will dive into advanced techniques such as cross-validation and ensemble methods to further refine your model's ability to generalize to new data.

Cross-Validation: Using Cross-Validation to Improve Model Robustness

Cross-validation is a powerful statistical method used to assess the robustness and generalizability of a model. By partitioning the dataset into multiple subsets and iteratively training and testing the model across these partitions, cross-validation provides a more comprehensive evaluation of model performance compared to a simple train-test split. This technique is especially valuable for deep learning and machine learning models where overfitting or underfitting is a concern.

In this section, we'll explore what cross-validation is, discuss the different types of cross-validation methods, and explain when and how to use them for training reliable deep learning models.

What is Cross-Validation?

Cross-validation divides the dataset into several parts, or "folds," then iteratively trains and tests the model across these folds. This allows the model to be evaluated on multiple "unseen" subsets of data, reducing the risk of overfitting and ensuring that the evaluation is not biased toward any particular subset of data.

The basic idea behind cross-validation is to ensure that each data point in the dataset gets a chance to be in the training set and the validation set. By doing so, it simulates multiple rounds of training and validation, giving a better indication of how the model will perform on entirely new data.

Why Use Cross-Validation?

Cross-validation addresses a few key challenges in model training:

- **Overfitting**: By evaluating the model on multiple subsets of the data, cross-validation helps reduce the likelihood that the model is merely memorizing patterns in the training data rather than learning generalizable features.
- **Performance Estimation**: Cross-validation gives a more accurate estimate of how the model is likely to perform on unseen data. This can lead to better choices in model selection and hyperparameter tuning.
- **Efficient Use of Data**: Especially with limited data, cross-validation makes optimal use of the dataset by training on multiple subsets rather than a single split.

Common Types of Cross-Validation

There are several methods of cross-validation, each with different strengths suited to specific data structures and goals. Here, we will discuss the most common methods and when to use them.

1. K-Fold Cross-Validation

K-Fold Cross-Validation is one of the most widely used cross-validation methods. In this technique, the dataset is split into K equally sized folds. The model is then trained and evaluated K times, each time using one fold as the validation set and the remaining $K-1$ folds as the training set. The average performance across all K trials gives the final assessment metric.

- **Step-by-Step Process**:

1. Divide the dataset into K folds.
2. For each fold, use it as a validation set and train the model on the remaining $K-1$ folds.
3. Calculate performance metrics (accuracy, precision, recall, etc.) for each iteration.
4. Average the metrics over all K folds to get a final evaluation.

- **When to Use**: K-Fold Cross-Validation works well for most datasets and is particularly useful when you have a moderate amount of data. A common choice is 5-fold or 10-fold cross-validation, with K values chosen to balance computational cost and robustness.

2. **Stratified K-Fold Cross-Validation**

Stratified K-Fold Cross-Validation is a variation of K-Fold where the data is split in such a way that each fold has the same proportion of each class as the original dataset. This ensures that all folds are representative of the overall class distribution, which is especially important when dealing with imbalanced datasets.

- **Step-by-Step Process**:

Divide the dataset into K folds, ensuring that each fold has the same class distribution as the entire dataset.

Proceed with K-Fold Cross-Validation as before.

- **When to Use**: This method is ideal for classification tasks, especially when there is a significant imbalance between classes, as it ensures that each fold contains a representative mix of classes.

3. Leave-One-Out Cross-Validation (LOOCV)

Leave-One-Out Cross-Validation (LOOCV) is an extreme case of K-Fold Cross-Validation where K is equal to the number of samples in the dataset. Each sample acts as its own validation set, while the model is trained on the remaining samples.

- **Step-by-Step Process**:

1. For each data point in the dataset, hold that single point out as the validation set.
2. Train the model on the remaining data points.
3. Repeat the process for each data point in the dataset.
4. Compute the average performance metric over all iterations.

- **When to Use**: LOOCV is generally not used for large datasets, as it can be computationally intensive. It is, however, suitable for small datasets where each data point is valuable, and the goal is to maximize the training data used in each iteration.

4. Time Series Cross-Validation

In **Time Series Cross-Validation**, the data is split with consideration of the temporal order. Instead of randomly selecting data points for each fold, this method uses the past data points to train the model and future data points to test it. This is often referred to as **Rolling Cross-Validation** or **Walk-Forward Validation**.

- **Step-by-Step Process**:

1. Split the data chronologically, starting with an initial subset of the data

as training data.

2. Train the model on the initial subset and evaluate it on the next "slice" of data.

3. Increase the training set by adding the next slice and re-evaluate.

4. Repeat this process until the entire dataset has been used.

- **When to Use**: This method is suitable for time series data or any dataset where maintaining the order of observations is crucial, such as financial forecasting, climate modeling, or any sequential data.

Practical Example of K-Fold Cross-Validation in Python

Below is a sample code snippet using K-Fold Cross-Validation with scikit-learn's KFold and a deep learning model created with Keras.

python

```
from sklearn.model_selection import KFold
from tensorflow.keras.models import Sequential
from tensorflow.keras.layers import Dense
import numpy as np

# Example dataset
X = np.random.rand(100, 10)  # 100 samples, 10 features
y = np.random.randint(0, 2, 100)  # Binary target

# Define a simple model
def create_model():
    model = Sequential([
        Dense(64, activation='relu', input_shape=(10,)),
        Dense(32, activation='relu'),
        Dense(1, activation='sigmoid')
    ])
    model.compile(optimizer='adam', loss='binary_crossentropy',
    metrics=['accuracy'])
    return model

# K-Fold Cross-Validation
```

```
k = 5
kf = KFold(n_splits=k, shuffle=True)
scores = []

for train_index, val_index in kf.split(X):
    X_train, X_val = X[train_index], X[val_index]
    y_train, y_val = y[train_index], y[val_index]

    model = create_model()
    model.fit(X_train, y_train, epochs=10, batch_size=8,
    verbose=0)

    # Evaluate on validation data
    score = model.evaluate(X_val, y_val, verbose=0)
    scores.append(score[1])  # Accuracy

print("Average accuracy over", k, "folds:", np.mean(scores))
```

Choosing the Right Cross-Validation Method

When choosing a cross-validation method, consider the size of your dataset, the structure of your data, and the computational resources available:

- **Small Datasets**: Consider LOOCV or K-Fold with a small K value to maximize training data.
- **Large Datasets**: Use K-Fold with higher K values for a balance between robustness and computational efficiency.
- **Imbalanced Classes**: Use Stratified K-Fold to ensure each fold is representative.
- **Sequential/Time Series Data**: Time Series Cross-Validation is best for preserving temporal dependencies.

215

Cross-validation is an essential tool for building robust, generalizable models. It mitigates the risks associated with overfitting, provides a more reliable estimate of model performance, and allows for optimal use of available data. By implementing cross-validation, you can ensure that your deep learning models are evaluated thoroughly and consistently across varying datasets and conditions. As we proceed, we will delve into more complex topics such as regularization techniques and hyperparameter tuning that further enhance model performance and reliability.

Fine-Tuning for Performance: Adjusting Learning Rates, Optimizers, and More

Fine-tuning deep learning models involves adjusting key hyperparameters and model settings to optimize performance. While training a neural network from scratch can yield good results, careful tuning can improve performance by allowing the model to learn more efficiently, adapt to specific data characteristics, and achieve higher accuracy.

In this section, we will explore the process of fine-tuning a model through adjustments to learning rates, optimizers, and additional settings such as learning rate schedules and momentum. Understanding and implementing these methods will enhance your ability to train more sophisticated, responsive models.

The Importance of Fine-Tuning in Deep Learning

In deep learning, fine-tuning is critical for the following reasons:

- **Maximizing Model Accuracy**: Small adjustments in hyperparameters can significantly affect the accuracy and loss metrics of a model.
- **Optimizing Training Speed**: Efficient hyperparameters reduce training time, making the model faster to train without sacrificing accuracy.
- **Avoiding Overfitting or Underfitting**: Fine-tuning can help in balancing the model's capacity to generalize, mitigating overfitting or underfitting based on dataset characteristics.

216

- **Efficient Resource Utilization**: Fine-tuned models often require less computational power by reaching optimal performance faster.

With this foundation, let's explore fine-tuning techniques, starting with learning rate adjustments.

Learning Rate: The Core Hyperparameter in Fine-Tuning

The learning rate is one of the most critical hyperparameters in neural network training. It controls the size of the steps taken by the optimization algorithm to minimize the loss function. A well-chosen learning rate ensures efficient convergence; however, setting it too high or too low can result in training inefficiencies.

- **High Learning Rates**: If set too high, the model may oscillate around the minimum or diverge entirely, as large steps make it difficult to zero in on the lowest loss values.
- **Low Learning Rates**: If set too low, the model might take too long to converge, or it may get stuck in local minima, resulting in suboptimal performance.

Techniques for Learning Rate Adjustment

1. **Manual Adjustment**: Manually testing various learning rates is a straightforward, trial-and-error approach, often starting with values like 0.001 or 0.0001 for gradient-based optimizers.
2. **Learning Rate Schedules**: These automated strategies adjust the learning rate over the course of training.

- **Step Decay**: Reduces the learning rate by a fixed factor (e.g., 0.5) after a set number of epochs. This approach works well for datasets with plateauing accuracy.
- **Exponential Decay**: Gradually decreases the learning rate by a factor at each epoch, allowing the model to converge more smoothly.

- **Reduce on Plateau**: Lowers the learning rate when a performance metric (e.g., validation loss) stalls. This adaptive method is especially useful in complex datasets where model performance varies.

```python
from tensorflow.keras.callbacks import ReduceLROnPlateau

lr_schedule = ReduceLROnPlateau(monitor='val_loss', factor=0.5,
patience=3, min_lr=1e-6)
model.fit(X_train, y_train, validation_data=(X_val, y_val),
epochs=50, callbacks=[lr_schedule])
```

Cyclical Learning Rates: Alternates between a lower and upper learning rate boundary, helping the model escape local minima by exploring various rates within a range. This approach is suitable for models that benefit from diverse learning rate values over time.

Optimizers: Choosing the Right Algorithm for Your Model

Optimizers control the manner and speed at which a model learns. Different optimizers have unique strengths that can significantly impact training efficiency and performance. Here's a brief overview of commonly used optimizers in deep learning and their best applications.

1. **Stochastic Gradient Descent (SGD)**: The foundational optimizer in neural networks, it updates weights based on each mini-batch's gradient. While SGD can be slow and prone to getting stuck in local minima, it works well with momentum adjustments.
2. **Momentum**: An extension of SGD, it adds a fraction of the previous update to the current one. This adjustment smooths out oscillations and accelerates convergence, particularly in sparse gradients.

```python
python

from tensorflow.keras.optimizers import SGD

optimizer = SGD(learning_rate=0.01, momentum=0.9)
model.compile(optimizer=optimizer, loss='binary_crossentropy',
metrics=['accuracy'])
```

1. **Adam (Adaptive Moment Estimation)**: A combination of RMSprop and momentum, Adam adapts the learning rate for each parameter based on first and second moments of gradients, making it efficient and stable. It's a versatile choice and often works well for most deep learning applications.
2. **RMSprop**: An adaptive learning rate method that works especially well for recurrent neural networks and time series data. RMSprop keeps a moving average of squared gradients, effectively controlling the learning rate for each parameter.

Additional Optimization Techniques

1. **Learning Rate Warmup**: Starts with a small learning rate that gradually increases until it reaches a predetermined value, after which it proceeds as normal. This technique helps stabilize training, especially with large datasets.
2. **Adaptive Gradient Clipping**: Prevents exploding gradients by clipping the gradient norms during backpropagation. Useful in RNNs and models prone to unstable gradient magnitudes.
3. **Early Stopping**: Halts training when the validation performance plateaus, which avoids unnecessary computations and reduces overfitting.

Practical Example: Fine-Tuning a Keras Model with Adam and Learning Rate Scheduling

Below is a code example demonstrating the setup of a model using Adam as the optimizer and a Reduce on Plateau schedule to adjust the learning rate during training:

```python
from tensorflow.keras.models import Sequential
from tensorflow.keras.layers import Dense
from tensorflow.keras.callbacks import ReduceLROnPlateau
from tensorflow.keras.optimizers import Adam

# Define model architecture
model = Sequential([
    Dense(128, activation='relu', input_shape=(10,)),
    Dense(64, activation='relu'),
    Dense(1, activation='sigmoid')
])

# Compile model with Adam optimizer
optimizer = Adam(learning_rate=0.001)
model.compile(optimizer=optimizer, loss='binary_crossentropy',
metrics=['accuracy'])

# Implement ReduceLROnPlateau for adaptive learning rate
lr_schedule = ReduceLROnPlateau(monitor='val_loss', factor=0.5,
patience=3, min_lr=1e-6)

# Fit the model with the learning rate schedule
model.fit(X_train, y_train, validation_data=(X_val, y_val),
epochs=50, callbacks=[lr_schedule])
```

Fine-Tuning and Model Generalization

Fine-tuning is essential not only for improving raw performance metrics but also for enhancing model generalization. A well-tuned model will likely perform consistently well across varied datasets, exhibiting resilience to overfitting. Moreover, fine-tuning reflects a balance between achieving high accuracy on the training data and ensuring that this performance translates to real-world data.

Fine-tuning a deep learning model involves a strategic approach to hyperparameter adjustment. By systematically altering learning rates, choosing the right optimizers, and implementing learning rate schedules, you can achieve a model that is not only accurate but also efficient and generalizable. Fine-tuning is an iterative process, requiring experimentation and continuous adjustment to identify the most effective settings for your specific dataset and task. As we move forward, we will look into further enhancing model performance through regularization techniques and various methods for handling overfitting.

Practical Projects and Real-World Case Studies

I mage Classification Project: **Building an Image Classifier from Dataset Collection to Model Deployment**

In this chapter, we'll walk through building a complete image classification project from start to finish, covering the essential stages: dataset collection, preprocessing, model selection, training, evaluation, and deployment. The objective of this project is to create a classifier that can categorize images into predefined classes. This workflow provides a hands-on understanding of practical model building and deployment in real-world applications, setting a strong foundation for similar projects across various domains.

Project Overview

Goal: Build an image classifier that can accurately predict labels for unseen images based on patterns learned during training.

Workflow:

1. Dataset Collection and Exploration
2. Data Preprocessing
3. Model Selection and Architecture Design
4. Model Training and Evaluation
5. Model Optimization and Fine-Tuning
6. Model Deployment

1. Dataset Collection and Exploration

A successful image classifier begins with a well-curated dataset. For this project, we'll use a publicly available dataset, such as CIFAR-10 or a similar set with multiple categories (e.g., animals, vehicles, objects).

- **Dataset Source**: Download from platforms like Kaggle, TensorFlow Datasets, or manually gather images if building a custom dataset.
- **Classes**: Define the categories. For example, if using CIFAR-10, classes could include airplane, car, bird, cat, deer, dog, frog, horse, ship, and truck.

Exploratory Data Analysis (EDA): Before preprocessing, explore the dataset by visualizing images from each class, understanding class distribution, and identifying potential challenges such as class imbalance or noisy images.

```python
import tensorflow as tf
import matplotlib.pyplot as plt

# Load dataset (example: CIFAR-10)
(x_train, y_train), (x_test, y_test) =
tf.keras.datasets.cifar10.load_data()

# Display sample images
fig, axes = plt.subplots(1, 5, figsize=(10, 10))
for i in range(5):
    axes[i].imshow(x_train[i])
    axes[i].axis('off')
plt.show()
```

2. Data Preprocessing

Data preprocessing is crucial to prepare the images for the neural network and improve model performance. Key steps include resizing, normalizing, augmenting, and dividing data into training, validation, and test sets.

223

- **Resizing and Rescaling**: Resize images to a consistent shape (e.g., 32x32 or 224x224) and scale pixel values to a range of 0-1.
- **Data Augmentation**: Introduce variability with transformations like rotations, flips, or brightness changes to enhance generalization.
- **Normalization**: Scale pixel values to improve convergence during training.

```python
python

from tensorflow.keras.preprocessing.image import
ImageDataGenerator

# Data augmentation and normalization
datagen = ImageDataGenerator(
    rescale=1.0/255.0,
    rotation_range=20,
    width_shift_range=0.1,
    height_shift_range=0.1,
    horizontal_flip=True,
    validation_split=0.2  # for validation data
)

# Fit on training data
train_gen = datagen.flow(x_train, y_train, batch_size=32,
subset='training')
val_gen = datagen.flow(x_train, y_train, batch_size=32,
subset='validation')
```

3. Model Selection and Architecture Design

For image classification, convolutional neural networks (CNNs) are the architecture of choice due to their ability to detect spatial patterns in images. Here, we can either build a CNN from scratch or leverage a pre-trained model like VGG16 or ResNet and fine-tune it for our dataset.

Building a Basic CNN Model

A basic CNN model consists of layers including convolutional, pooling, and fully connected layers. This structure captures essential image features and maps them to class probabilities.

python

```
from tensorflow.keras.models import Sequential
from tensorflow.keras.layers import Conv2D, MaxPooling2D,
Flatten, Dense

# Define the CNN model
model = Sequential([
    Conv2D(32, (3, 3), activation='relu', input_shape=(32, 32,
    3)),
    MaxPooling2D((2, 2)),
    Conv2D(64, (3, 3), activation='relu'),
    MaxPooling2D((2, 2)),
    Conv2D(128, (3, 3), activation='relu'),
    Flatten(),
    Dense(128, activation='relu'),
    Dense(10, activation='softmax')  # 10 classes for CIFAR-10
])

# Compile the model
model.compile(optimizer='adam',
loss='sparse_categorical_crossentropy', metrics=['accuracy'])
```

Using Transfer Learning

If the dataset is small or if rapid prototyping is desired, using a pre-trained model like VGG16, ResNet50, or MobileNet can save time and improve accuracy.

python

```
from tensorflow.keras.applications import VGG16

# Load the pre-trained model with weights trained on ImageNet
base_model = VGG16(input_shape=(224, 224, 3), include_top=False,
```

```
weights='imagenet')

# Add custom layers on top of base model
model = Sequential([
    base_model,
    Flatten(),
    Dense(256, activation='relu'),
    Dense(10, activation='softmax')
])

# Freeze the base model layers
for layer in base_model.layers:
    layer.trainable = False

model.compile(optimizer='adam',
loss='sparse_categorical_crossentropy', metrics=['accuracy'])
```

4. Model Training and Evaluation

Train the model on the training dataset while monitoring its performance on the validation set. Model evaluation allows us to track accuracy, loss, and other metrics to understand how well the model generalizes.

- **Training**: Use the fit() function in TensorFlow or Keras, setting epochs based on dataset size and model complexity.
- **Validation**: Track performance on validation data to tune hyperparameters and avoid overfitting.

```python
# Train the model
history = model.fit(train_gen, epochs=20, validation_data=val_gen)
```

5. Model Optimization and Fine-Tuning

To enhance model performance, apply optimization techniques like adjusting the learning rate, using more sophisticated optimizers, or fine-tuning the pre-trained layers.

- **Fine-Tuning Pre-trained Models**: Unfreeze some top layers of the pre-trained model and retrain them on our dataset.
- **Learning Rate Scheduling**: Reduce learning rates progressively to improve convergence.

```python
python

# Fine-tune some layers
for layer in model.layers[-5:]:
    layer.trainable = True

# Recompile and retrain
model.compile(optimizer=tf.keras.optimizers.Adam(learning_rate=0.0001),
loss='sparse_categorical_crossentropy', metrics=['accuracy'])
history = model.fit(train_gen, epochs=10, validation_data=val_gen)
```

6. Model Deployment

Once training and fine-tuning are complete, the final step is deploying the model so it can be used in real-world applications. Deployment can involve saving the model, creating an API, or integrating it into a mobile or web application.

Saving and Exporting the Model

Save the trained model to load it later or deploy it on different platforms. TensorFlow and Keras provide straightforward methods for saving models, which can then be loaded for inference.

```python
python

# Save the trained model
model.save('image_classifier_model.h5')
```

Creating an API for Model Inference

For practical use, create an API endpoint to serve the model, allowing external applications to make predictions on new images. Using frameworks like Flask or FastAPI, you can deploy the model as a service.

```python
python

# Example using Flask (simple pseudocode)
from flask import Flask, request, jsonify
import tensorflow as tf

app = Flask(__name__)
model = tf.keras.models.load_model('image_classifier_model.h5')

@app.route('/predict', methods=['POST'])
def predict():
    # Code to process incoming image and return prediction
    return jsonify(prediction=pred_class)

if __name__ == '__main__':
    app.run()
```

Building an image classifier is a comprehensive task involving dataset selection, preprocessing, model architecture design, training, and deployment. This hands-on project serves as a robust example of how to approach deep learning tasks with structured steps. Through the process of developing, training, and deploying this image classifier, we've explored essential deep learning practices that lay the groundwork for tackling more advanced projects. As we continue, we will delve into handling more complex image data and enhancing model capabilities through advanced deep learning techniques.

Text Classification with RNNs: Sentiment Analysis on Real-World Datasets

Text classification is a foundational task in natural language processing (NLP), and sentiment analysis is one of its most widely used applications. Sentiment analysis seeks to determine the emotional tone behind a series of words, commonly categorizing text into positive, negative, or neutral sentiments. Recurrent neural networks (RNNs) excel in this domain due to their ability to handle sequence data, remembering contextual information in sequences and making them particularly suited for language-related tasks. In this section, we'll develop an RNN-based model for sentiment analysis using real-world text datasets.

Overview of Sentiment Analysis

Goal: Build a sentiment analysis classifier capable of determining the polarity (positive, negative, neutral) of text inputs, such as movie reviews, product feedback, or social media comments.

Dataset: We'll use a well-known sentiment analysis dataset, such as the IMDb movie review dataset, which contains thousands of labeled movie reviews categorized as positive or negative. This dataset is available in the TensorFlow and Keras libraries, or it can be downloaded from platforms like Kaggle.

1. Preparing the Dataset

First, load and preprocess the text data. Text preprocessing typically involves tokenization, padding, and vectorization to make the data compatible with neural network models.

- **Tokenization**: Convert words into numerical tokens.
- **Padding**: Ensure each sequence is the same length by padding shorter sequences, helping the model to process inputs uniformly.
- **Splitting**: Divide the dataset into training and validation sets to evaluate performance during training.

229

```python
python

from tensorflow.keras.datasets import imdb
from tensorflow.keras.preprocessing.sequence import pad_sequences

# Load IMDb dataset
max_words = 10000  # number of words to consider as features
(x_train, y_train), (x_val, y_val) =
imdb.load_data(num_words=max_words)

# Pad sequences to ensure uniform length
maxlen = 200  # max length of input sequences
x_train = pad_sequences(x_train, maxlen=maxlen)
x_val = pad_sequences(x_val, maxlen=maxlen)
```

2. Building the RNN Model

For text classification tasks, we can use RNN variants like LSTMs (Long Short-Term Memory networks) or GRUs (Gated Recurrent Units), which are designed to capture long-term dependencies and contextual relationships in sequences.

Model Architecture

The architecture of a sentiment analysis model often includes an embedding layer, an RNN layer (LSTM or GRU), and fully connected layers. The embedding layer converts integer tokens into dense vectors of fixed size, providing a more nuanced representation of words.

```python
python

from tensorflow.keras.models import Sequential
from tensorflow.keras.layers import Embedding, LSTM, Dense

# Define the RNN model
model = Sequential([
    Embedding(input_dim=max_words, output_dim=128,
    input_length=maxlen),
```

```
    LSTM(64, dropout=0.2, recurrent_dropout=0.2),
    Dense(1, activation='sigmoid')  # binary classification:
    positive or negative sentiment
])

# Compile the model
model.compile(optimizer='adam', loss='binary_crossentropy',
metrics=['accuracy'])
```

3. Training the Model

With the model defined, the next step is to train it on the IMDb dataset. The goal is to allow the RNN to learn patterns in word sequences that correlate with positive or negative sentiment.

- **Batch Size**: Set to a manageable size (e.g., 32 or 64) to balance computational load and convergence speed.
- **Epochs**: Use a sufficient number of epochs, typically between 5-10 for text-based tasks.

```python
# Train the model
history = model.fit(
    x_train, y_train,
    epochs=10,
    batch_size=64,
    validation_data=(x_val, y_val)
)
```

4. Evaluating Model Performance

Once trained, evaluate the model on the validation set to assess its accuracy, loss, and generalization. Common metrics for classification tasks include accuracy, precision, recall, and F1 score. If accuracy meets the target performance, the model is ready for further fine-tuning or deployment.

python

```
# Evaluate the model
loss, accuracy = model.evaluate(x_val, y_val)
print(f"Validation Loss: {loss}")
print(f"Validation Accuracy: {accuracy}")
```

5. Practical Considerations and Improvements

For improved performance, consider additional strategies such as:

- **Hyperparameter Tuning**: Experiment with different hyperparameters, such as the number of LSTM units, dropout rates, and learning rates, to optimize accuracy.
- **Regularization**: Techniques like dropout are already in use but can be adjusted to reduce overfitting further.
- **Bidirectional RNNs**: For some sentiment analysis tasks, using bidirectional RNNs, which process sequences both forward and backward, can improve accuracy.

This text classification project provides a foundation in building RNN-based sentiment analysis models for real-world applications. By leveraging sequential data capabilities, this RNN model can accurately classify text based on sentiment, making it applicable to a wide range of domains, from customer feedback analysis to automated content moderation. In subsequent projects, expanding the architecture with attention mechanisms or transformer models could further enhance performance on complex NLP tasks.

Time-Series Forecasting: Using LSTMs for Stock Price Prediction and Sequential Data

Time-series forecasting is essential across fields like finance, healthcare, weather prediction, and supply chain management. Long Short-Term

Memory networks (LSTMs) are especially effective for this task due to their ability to capture dependencies over long sequences, making them well-suited to sequential data with temporal patterns. In this section, we'll focus on using LSTMs for stock price prediction, a classic example of time-series forecasting.

Overview of Time-Series Forecasting with LSTMs

In time-series forecasting, the goal is to predict future values based on historical data. For stock price prediction, this typically involves predicting future prices based on past prices, volumes, and possibly other indicators.

- **Objective**: Build an LSTM-based model that predicts future stock prices based on historical price data.
- **Dataset**: For this tutorial, we'll use historical stock prices from a dataset like Yahoo Finance or an open dataset available on Kaggle.

1. Preparing the Dataset

Before feeding data into the LSTM model, the time-series data needs preprocessing, including scaling, reshaping, and splitting into training and test sets.

1. **Load Data**: Load historical stock price data. Data should include daily closing prices or adjusted closing prices.
2. **Feature Scaling**: Normalize the data using techniques like Min-Max scaling to ensure all values fall between 0 and 1. This scaling helps with model convergence.
3. **Sequence Creation**: Create sequences for the model, where each sequence contains a window of past prices that the LSTM will use to predict the next price.

python

```
import numpy as np
import pandas as pd
from sklearn.preprocessing import MinMaxScaler

# Load data
data = pd.read_csv('path_to_stock_data.csv')  # Replace with your
data file
closing_prices = data['Close'].values  # Use closing price for
simplicity
closing_prices = closing_prices.reshape(-1, 1)

# Scale the data
scaler = MinMaxScaler(feature_range=(0, 1))
scaled_data = scaler.fit_transform(closing_prices)

# Create sequences for training
def create_sequences(data, sequence_length=60):
    x, y = [], []
    for i in range(sequence_length, len(data)):
        x.append(data[i-sequence_length:i, 0])
        y.append(data[i, 0])
    return np.array(x), np.array(y)

sequence_length = 60  # Predict based on the previous 60 days
x, y = create_sequences(scaled_data, sequence_length)
x = np.reshape(x, (x.shape[0], x.shape[1], 1))  # Reshape for
LSTM input
```

2. Building the LSTM Model

LSTM layers are particularly useful for capturing patterns in time-series data, as they can remember and learn from sequences of past values. A basic LSTM model for stock prediction may contain one or more LSTM layers followed by dense layers.

Model Architecture

- **Input Shape**: (sequence_length, 1), where sequence_length is the number of days used for each prediction window.
- **Layers**: An LSTM layer followed by a dense layer to produce a single

output.

```python
from tensorflow.keras.models import Sequential
from tensorflow.keras.layers import LSTM, Dense, Dropout

# Define the LSTM model
model = Sequential([
    LSTM(50, return_sequences=True, input_shape=(sequence_length,
    1)),
    Dropout(0.2),
    LSTM(50, return_sequences=False),
    Dropout(0.2),
    Dense(25),
    Dense(1)  # Predict a single price
])

# Compile the model
model.compile(optimizer='adam', loss='mean_squared_error')
```

3. Training the Model

Once the model architecture is defined, we can train it using the prepared time-series data. The training process involves passing sequences of past prices and minimizing the mean squared error (MSE) between the predicted and actual prices.

- **Batch Size**: Smaller batch sizes, such as 32 or 64, work well for time-series data.
- **Epochs**: A higher number of epochs, around 50-100, may be needed due to the complexity of the data.

```python
```

```
# Train the model
history = model.fit(x, y, epochs=50, batch_size=64,
validation_split=0.2)
```

4. Making Predictions and Evaluating Model Performance

After training, the model can be used to predict future stock prices. To evaluate, we'll measure the model's performance using mean squared error (MSE) and visualize predicted vs. actual stock prices.

1. **Prepare Test Data**: Use recent data that the model hasn't seen during training.
2. **Inverse Transform**: To interpret predictions in the original price scale, apply the inverse of the scaling transformation.

python

```
# Predicting future stock prices
predicted_prices = model.predict(x_test)
predicted_prices = scaler.inverse_transform(predicted_prices)  #
Scale back to original prices

# Visualizing the predictions
import matplotlib.pyplot as plt

plt.figure(figsize=(12, 6))
plt.plot(real_prices, color='blue', label='Actual Stock Price')
plt.plot(predicted_prices, color='red', label='Predicted Stock
Price')
plt.title('Stock Price Prediction')
plt.xlabel('Time')
plt.ylabel('Stock Price')
plt.legend()
plt.show()
```

5. Practical Considerations and Improvements

- **Hyperparameter Tuning**: Experiment with sequence length, batch size, and number of epochs to find the optimal configuration for the dataset.
- **Adding Additional Features**: Improve model accuracy by incorporating other indicators (volume, moving averages) as additional input features.
- **Using Advanced Architectures**: Explore bidirectional LSTMs or GRUs for potentially enhanced results.

Time-series forecasting with LSTMs opens up powerful predictive capabilities for sequential data. By understanding historical patterns, our LSTM-based stock price prediction model can make informed predictions about future trends. This methodology extends beyond finance and can be applied to various domains, offering robust solutions for forecasting and decision-making.

Hands-On with GANs for Image Synthesis: Generating Synthetic Images for Various Applications

Generative Adversarial Networks (GANs) have revolutionized the field of artificial intelligence, particularly in image synthesis and data generation. They consist of two neural networks—the **generator** and the **discriminator**—that work in opposition to one another to create realistic synthetic data. This section offers a hands-on guide to building a basic GAN for image synthesis, covering the fundamental steps of model creation, training, and image generation.

Introduction to GANs

GANs are a type of deep learning model developed by Ian Goodfellow in 2014. They operate on the principle of adversarial learning, where the generator tries to create realistic images, and the discriminator tries to differentiate between real and synthetic images. Over time, the generator learns to produce increasingly realistic images that can "fool" the discriminator.

- **Generator**: Produces synthetic data (e.g., images) from random noise.
- **Discriminator**: Tries to distinguish between real data and data produced by the generator.

Applications of GANs in Image Synthesis

GANs are widely used for:

- **Image Super-Resolution**: Enhancing the resolution of images.
- **Art and Content Creation**: Creating new art pieces, animations, and textures.
- **Data Augmentation**: Generating synthetic samples to expand datasets for machine learning tasks.
- **Medical Imaging**: Producing synthetic images for training and testing models in healthcare.

1. Setting Up the Environment

To implement a GAN, we need Python libraries like TensorFlow and Keras. For our example, we'll use the MNIST dataset, a popular collection of handwritten digit images, to demonstrate image synthesis.

```python
# Import libraries
import numpy as np
import tensorflow as tf
from tensorflow.keras.layers import Dense, Reshape, Flatten,
BatchNormalization, LeakyReLU
from tensorflow.keras.models import Sequential
from tensorflow.keras.datasets import mnist
import matplotlib.pyplot as plt
```

2. Preparing the Data

For this tutorial, we'll use the MNIST dataset, which consists of 28x28 grayscale images of handwritten digits. The generator will create synthetic images resembling these digits.

python

```
# Load and preprocess the data
(x_train, _), (_, _) = mnist.load_data()
x_train = (x_train - 127.5) / 127.5  # Normalize to [-1, 1]
x_train = np.expand_dims(x_train, axis=3)  # Reshape to (28, 28,
1)
```

3. Building the Generator Network

The generator's role is to take random noise as input and output a synthetic image. The model uses upsampling layers to produce images of 28x28 pixels.

python

```
def build_generator():
    model = Sequential([
        Dense(256, input_dim=100),
        LeakyReLU(alpha=0.2),
        BatchNormalization(momentum=0.8),
        Dense(512),
        LeakyReLU(alpha=0.2),
        BatchNormalization(momentum=0.8),
        Dense(1024),
        LeakyReLU(alpha=0.2),
        BatchNormalization(momentum=0.8),
        Dense(28 * 28 * 1, activation='tanh'),
        Reshape((28, 28, 1))
    ])
    return model
```

The input is a 100-dimensional noise vector, which is transformed through dense layers and activated with **LeakyReLU**. Finally, it reshapes the output into a 28x28 pixel image.

4. Building the Discriminator Network

The discriminator's role is to classify images as real or fake. It takes a 28x28 image as input and outputs a binary classification indicating whether the image is real or generated.

python

```python
def build_discriminator():
    model = Sequential([
        Flatten(input_shape=(28, 28, 1)),
        Dense(512),
        LeakyReLU(alpha=0.2),
        Dense(256),
        LeakyReLU(alpha=0.2),
        Dense(1, activation='sigmoid')
    ])
    return model
```

The discriminator flattens the input image and passes it through dense layers, using **LeakyReLU** activations to capture non-linear relationships.

5. Compiling the GAN

The GAN consists of both networks connected sequentially. The generator attempts to create images that can trick the discriminator, and the discriminator is trained to identify whether an image is real or generated.

python

```python
# Build and compile the discriminator
discriminator = build_discriminator()
discriminator.compile(loss='binary_crossentropy',
optimizer='adam', metrics=['accuracy'])

# Build the generator
generator = build_generator()

# Connect them to form the GAN
```

```
gan = Sequential([generator, discriminator])

# Freeze discriminator layers for the combined model
discriminator.trainable = False
gan.compile(loss='binary_crossentropy', optimizer='adam')
```

Here, we compile the discriminator independently to allow it to classify real and fake images accurately. For the GAN model, the discriminator's weights are frozen to focus training on the generator.

6. Training the GAN

Training a GAN involves iteratively training the generator and discriminator in a two-part process:

1. **Train Discriminator**: Real images from the dataset and generated images from the generator are used to train the discriminator.
2. **Train Generator**: The generator's weights are updated to maximize the discriminator's error when distinguishing fake images.

python

```
def train_gan(epochs=10000, batch_size=128, sample_interval=1000):
    real = np.ones((batch_size, 1))
    fake = np.zeros((batch_size, 1))

    for epoch in range(epochs):
        # Train discriminator
        idx = np.random.randint(0, x_train.shape[0], batch_size)
        real_imgs = x_train[idx]

        noise = np.random.normal(0, 1, (batch_size, 100))
        gen_imgs = generator.predict(noise)

        d_loss_real = discriminator.train_on_batch(real_imgs,
```

```
real)
d_loss_fake = discriminator.train_on_batch(gen_imgs, fake)
d_loss = 0.5 * np.add(d_loss_real, d_loss_fake)

# Train generator
noise = np.random.normal(0, 1, (batch_size, 100))
g_loss = gan.train_on_batch(noise, real)

# Display progress and save generated samples
if epoch % sample_interval == 0:
    print(f"{epoch} [D loss: {d_loss[0]}, acc.: {100 *
    d_loss[1]}] [G loss: {g_loss}]")
    sample_images(epoch)
```

7. Visualizing Generated Images

To evaluate the quality of images produced by the generator, we periodically visualize generated images during training.

python

```
def sample_images(epoch, image_grid_rows=5, image_grid_columns=5):
    noise = np.random.normal(0, 1, (image_grid_rows *
    image_grid_columns, 100))
    gen_imgs = generator.predict(noise)
    gen_imgs = 0.5 * gen_imgs + 0.5  # Rescale images to [0, 1]

    fig, axs = plt.subplots(image_grid_rows, image_grid_columns,
    figsize=(10, 10))
    count = 0
    for i in range(image_grid_rows):
        for j in range(image_grid_columns):
            axs[i, j].imshow(gen_imgs[count, :, :, 0],
            cmap='gray')
            axs[i, j].axis('off')
            count += 1
    plt.show()
```

This function generates a grid of images by sampling random noise and passing it through the generator, allowing us to observe improvements in image quality as training progresses.

This GAN-based approach for image synthesis illustrates how deep learning can create realistic images from random noise. Through adversarial training, the generator learns to create images closely resembling real data. GANs have extensive applications, from creating synthetic datasets to generating art, improving image resolution, and enhancing various fields where realistic synthetic data is beneficial.

Real-World Case Studies: Industry-Specific Applications of Deep Learning

Deep learning has profoundly impacted multiple industries by enabling more efficient, accurate, and innovative solutions. Here, we delve into a few notable case studies demonstrating how deep learning is applied across fields such as **medical image analysis**, **language translation**, and **autonomous driving**. Each case study highlights specific challenges and benefits, showcasing the transformative power of deep learning in real-world scenarios.

Medical Image Analysis

Context and Challenge: Medical imaging, a cornerstone of modern diagnostics, generates vast amounts of data in forms like X-rays, MRIs, and CT scans. Interpreting these images accurately and efficiently is crucial, yet this task is often time-consuming and error-prone, even for specialists.

Solution with Deep Learning: Deep learning algorithms, especially Convolutional Neural Networks (CNNs), excel in analyzing image data, making them ideal for medical applications. CNNs can be trained on labeled medical images to identify abnormalities like tumors, fractures, and signs of diseases. One prominent example is **lung cancer detection**. Lung cancer detection systems, trained on thousands of lung scan images, can identify suspicious nodules with a high degree of accuracy, even in early stages that may be challenging for human radiologists to spot.

Example Application – Google DeepMind's Eye Disease Diagnosis: In collaboration with Moorfields Eye Hospital, DeepMind developed a deep learning model to diagnose over 50 different eye diseases by analyzing retinal scans. The model's diagnostic accuracy rivals that of human experts, offering not only speed but also a second opinion in complex cases. This model helps prioritize high-risk patients, allowing quicker interventions and better outcomes.

Benefits:

- **Increased Accuracy**: Deep learning models often match or exceed human diagnostic capabilities.
- **Efficiency**: Processing large datasets quickly enables faster diagnostics and patient triage.
- **Scalability**: Models can be deployed across various medical centers, making advanced diagnostics accessible in regions lacking specialists.

Language Translation

Context and Challenge: Language translation is essential for communication, especially in a globalized world. Traditional rule-based or statistical translation methods have limited flexibility, often failing to capture nuanced meanings and contexts accurately. Deep learning offers a breakthrough with **transformers** and **sequence-to-sequence models**.

Solution with Deep Learning: The **Transformer model**, a deep learning architecture, was designed to improve language understanding by focusing on the concept of **attention mechanisms**. Attention allows the model to weigh different parts of a sentence based on context, greatly enhancing translation accuracy. Transformers can generate more fluent and contextually appropriate translations by learning relationships between words and phrases within sentences.

Example Application – Google Translate's Neural Machine Trans-

lation (NMT): Google implemented NMT, powered by Transformer architecture, to replace its earlier phrase-based systems. This upgrade significantly improved the quality of translations by generating contextually accurate sentences, especially in complex languages and linguistic structures. For instance, when translating between languages like Japanese and English, the model captures idiomatic expressions and grammatical differences more effectively.

Benefits:

- **Contextual Accuracy**: Attention mechanisms allow models to understand sentence context, reducing mistranslations.
- **Versatility**: Supports a wide array of languages and can be further trained on specialized vocabulary for industry-specific translations.
- **Continuous Improvement**: NMT models improve over time as they receive feedback and additional training data.

Autonomous Driving

Context and Challenge: Self-driving cars represent one of the most advanced and complex applications of AI and deep learning. Autonomous driving systems must interpret data from sensors, make split-second decisions, and navigate safely under various conditions. The main challenges include handling unpredictable environments, ensuring passenger safety, and meeting regulatory standards.

Solution with Deep Learning: Deep learning plays a key role in processing and interpreting sensor data. **Convolutional Neural Networks (CNNs)** are commonly used for visual recognition tasks, while **Recurrent Neural Networks (RNNs)** and **Reinforcement Learning** help the system make sequential decisions based on the car's current state. Autonomous vehicles integrate data from cameras, LiDAR, radar, and other sensors to recognize objects (e.g., pedestrians, other vehicles, road signs) and understand their surroundings.

Example Application – Tesla's Full Self-Driving (FSD) System: Tesla's FSD uses a neural network trained on massive datasets from real-world driving scenarios. The network processes visual data to recognize objects, predict their movement, and navigate safely through traffic. Tesla's approach emphasizes **end-to-end learning**, allowing the system to learn from extensive driving experience rather than predefined rules.

Benefits:

- **Enhanced Safety**: Deep learning models improve hazard detection and reaction times, potentially reducing human error.
- **Adaptability**: Models can handle dynamic environments and evolve with new data, making them suitable for diverse driving conditions.
- **Efficiency**: Autonomous driving reduces the need for manual driving, allowing passengers to focus on other tasks and optimizing route planning.

These case studies illustrate the versatility of deep learning across various fields. From medical diagnostics to language translation and autonomous driving, deep learning provides scalable, adaptable solutions that drive innovation and improve efficiency in real-world applications. By leveraging deep learning, industries are pushing the boundaries of what's possible, paving the way for advancements that were once thought out of reach.

Deploying Deep Learning Models

Deployment Basics: **Exporting Models and Understanding Deployment Environments**

Deploying a deep learning model is a crucial step in moving from experimentation to practical, real-world applications. Deployment ensures that a trained model can interact with live data and deliver results in various settings, whether it's a web app, mobile device, or edge device like an IoT sensor. This section focuses on the basics of model deployment, covering model export, key considerations for deployment environments, and strategies for efficient deployment in different contexts.

1. Model Export: Preparing Models for Deployment

The initial step in deployment is exporting the trained model, making it ready to integrate with different applications. Popular deep learning frameworks like TensorFlow, PyTorch, and Keras provide tools and formats to facilitate smooth model export.

Common Export Formats

1. **TensorFlow SavedModel**: The SavedModel format is a universal serialization format for TensorFlow models. It includes the model architecture, weights, and optimizer states, making it easy to load and deploy across TensorFlow environments. This format is particularly suitable for cloud deployment, as many cloud services support it natively.

2. **ONNX (Open Neural Network Exchange)**: ONNX is an open-

source format designed to enable interoperability across different machine learning frameworks, including PyTorch, TensorFlow, and Caffe. Using ONNX, you can export a model from PyTorch and then deploy it in a TensorFlow or other compatible environment, making it highly flexible for cross-framework compatibility.

3. **HDF5 and JSON (for Keras Models)**: Keras models can be saved in HDF5 (for both architecture and weights) or JSON (for architecture only) formats. While HDF5 saves all information needed for deployment, JSON files require the model's weights to be saved separately.

4. **TorchScript (for PyTorch Models)**: TorchScript is PyTorch's intermediate representation, which allows you to save a model in a format compatible with other programming languages, enabling easier deployment on mobile or embedded devices.

Model Export Process

The process of exporting a model generally involves three steps:

- **Saving the Model**: Use your framework's API (e.g., model.save() in Keras, torch.save() in PyTorch) to export the model in the desired format.
- **Testing the Exported Model**: Once exported, it's essential to test the saved model on sample data to ensure that it produces consistent results as during training.
- **Documenting Model Metadata**: When exporting a model, document any important metadata, such as input dimensions, pre-processing steps, and output labels, to ensure the deployment system can correctly interpret the model. Proper documentation of metadata is crucial, as it helps maintain consistency in model performance across different environments. This includes information on input and output shapes, expected data formats, preprocessing requirements, and any dependencies the model relies on.

2. Understanding Deployment Environments

Choosing the right environment for deploying a model depends on various factors, including the use case, required response time, hardware availability, and system constraints. Broadly, deployment environments fall into three categories:

A. Cloud-Based Deployment

Cloud environments are ideal for large-scale, high-availability applications that require significant computing power and scalability. Cloud providers like AWS, Google Cloud, and Azure offer managed services specifically for machine learning models, making it easy to deploy and scale applications on demand.

- **Pros**: High scalability, easy integration with data pipelines, access to powerful hardware (GPUs, TPUs), and managed services like AWS SageMaker, Google AI Platform, and Azure Machine Learning.
- **Cons**: Higher costs, especially for continuous high-volume requests; potential latency issues depending on geographical location.

Example Use Cases:

- Real-time image analysis for web applications
- Natural language processing models for chatbots and virtual assistants
- Predictive analytics in a business intelligence dashboard

B. On-Premises Deployment

On-premises deployment involves running the model on local hardware, such as servers or specialized devices within an organization's infrastructure. This approach is common in industries with strict data privacy requirements (e.g., healthcare, finance) where data cannot be easily shared with cloud providers.

- **Pros**: Greater data security, control over hardware resources, lower latency as data remains within the local network.

- **Cons**: Limited scalability, hardware constraints, and higher maintenance overhead as resources are managed internally.

Example Use Cases:

- Healthcare diagnostics using sensitive patient data
- Financial fraud detection within an organization's data center
- Industrial equipment monitoring and fault detection

C. Edge Deployment

Edge deployment places the model directly on devices like mobile phones, IoT sensors, or embedded systems, enabling predictions close to the data source. This setup is particularly useful for applications requiring low latency and minimal reliance on internet connectivity.

- **Pros**: Extremely low latency, no need for constant internet access, improved user privacy as data remains on the device.
- **Cons**: Limited computational power, often requiring model compression or optimization techniques to fit on resource-constrained devices.

Example Use Cases:

- Autonomous vehicles and real-time navigation
- Smart home devices for personalized recommendations
- Wearable health devices analyzing real-time health metrics

3. Deployment Considerations

To ensure smooth deployment, it's essential to account for several practical aspects. Each deployment scenario has unique requirements and limitations, so these considerations can help optimize model performance and ensure reliability.

A. Model Optimization

For effective deployment, especially on edge devices, models often need to be optimized to reduce their memory footprint and computational demand. Common techniques include:

- **Quantization**: Reducing the precision of model weights (e.g., from 32-bit to 8-bit) to decrease memory usage without significantly affecting accuracy.
- **Pruning**: Removing redundant parameters, such as less important neurons or filters, to make the model lighter and faster.
- **Knowledge Distillation**: Training a smaller, less complex model (student model) using predictions from a larger, more complex model (teacher model) to retain much of the accuracy in a smaller footprint.

B. Latency and Throughput

Different applications have different latency and throughput requirements. For example, a real-time application such as video processing requires minimal latency, while batch processing for recommendation engines can afford higher latency. Cloud and on-premises deployments can handle high-throughput needs more effectively, while edge deployments are suited for low-latency requirements.

C. Security and Privacy

When deploying models, particularly in sensitive domains like healthcare or finance, securing both the model and data is paramount. Consider using encryption methods to protect data in transit and at rest, and take steps to guard against model inversion attacks, where adversaries attempt to reconstruct the training data from the model's outputs.

D. Monitoring and Maintenance

Models need ongoing monitoring to ensure they continue to perform as expected in production. Model drift—where a model's accuracy decreases over time due to changes in input data or context—requires special attention. Implement monitoring tools to track performance metrics and set up alerts if accuracy drops below a certain threshold, signaling when retraining might be necessary.

4. Exporting Models for Different Deployment Scenarios

Here's a quick guide for exporting models tailored to specific deployment setups:

- **For Cloud-Based Deployment**: Use formats like TensorFlow Saved-Model or PyTorch TorchScript, and consider integrating with cloud-specific APIs or managed services like AWS Lambda for serverless deployments.
- **For On-Premises Deployment**: Export using ONNX for cross-framework compatibility, enabling seamless integration into custom servers. Implement monitoring solutions locally to track and optimize performance.
- **For Edge Deployment**: Use lightweight formats and optimization techniques to minimize size and computational load. TensorFlow Lite and ONNX are popular choices for mobile and embedded applications, while models can also be converted to CoreML for Apple devices.

5. Testing and Validating Deployed Models

Before fully launching a model in a production environment, perform thorough testing to ensure consistent and reliable performance. Key testing methods include:

- **A/B Testing**: Deploy multiple model versions to evaluate their performance against each other, selecting the best-performing model based on metrics like accuracy, response time, or user satisfaction.
- **Stress Testing**: Evaluate the model's performance under high load conditions, ensuring it can handle expected traffic volume without significant performance degradation.
- **User Acceptance Testing (UAT)**: Engage end-users to test the model in real-world scenarios, gathering feedback on its effectiveness, usability,

and reliability.

Deploying a deep learning model involves careful planning, understanding the target environment, and optimizing the model to fit real-world constraints. By selecting the appropriate deployment strategy—whether cloud, on-premises, or edge—and using export formats like SavedModel, ONNX, and TensorFlow Lite, developers can ensure their models are robust and effective. Additionally, with techniques like quantization, model monitoring, and security measures in place, deployed models remain optimized and secure, delivering accurate predictions and actionable insights in diverse settings.

Model deployment is the final, crucial step to realizing the potential of deep learning in practical applications, transforming prototypes into powerful, accessible tools that bring value to businesses and users alike.

Web and Mobile Deployment: Tools and Techniques for Deploying Models to Web and Mobile Apps

Deploying deep learning models to web and mobile applications requires tailored tools and strategies to ensure that models perform optimally on various devices and operating systems. Web and mobile deployment makes AI accessible to a vast audience, enabling applications from real-time image processing to personalized recommendations. Here, we'll cover popular tools, best practices, and deployment techniques for web and mobile platforms.

1. Web Deployment: Integrating Models into Web Applications

Web deployment offers easy accessibility to users through a browser interface, making it ideal for applications that don't require powerful local hardware. There are two main approaches to web deployment: server-side deployment and client-side (or in-browser) deployment. Each approach has unique benefits and challenges.

A. Server-Side Deployment

In server-side deployment, the model runs on a server, and client devices send data requests to the server, which processes the data using the model and returns predictions.

Key Tools and Frameworks:

- **Flask/Django (Python Web Frameworks)**: Flask and Django can serve models as RESTful APIs. Flask is lightweight and flexible, while Django offers more built-in functionality. These frameworks are commonly used to create web applications or APIs that handle HTTP requests, pass data to the model, and return results to the user.

- **FastAPI**: Known for its speed and simplicity, FastAPI is designed for serving machine learning models at scale. It supports asynchronous requests, which is advantageous for applications requiring high concurrency.

- **TensorFlow Serving**: TensorFlow Serving is optimized for serving TensorFlow models in production. It provides features for versioned model management and fast inference, making it a great choice for scaling.

- **TorchServe**: Developed by AWS and Facebook, TorchServe is an open-source tool for serving PyTorch models. It supports deployment of multiple models, versioning, and even GPU acceleration for faster predictions.

Benefits and Considerations:

- **Scalability**: Server-side deployment is highly scalable and can handle multiple requests simultaneously.
- **Security**: Model and data processing remain on the server, allowing for more secure handling of sensitive data.
- **Latency**: Server-side deployment may introduce latency due to data transfer between client and server, especially when handling large requests or high traffic.

Example Use Cases:

- Real-time language translation services
- Web-based recommendation systems
- Online object detection applications in e-commerce

B. Client-Side Deployment (In-Browser)

Client-side deployment enables models to run directly in the user's browser, removing the need for a server to process requests. This approach is particularly useful for applications requiring low latency and high interactivity, as it processes data locally on the client's device.

Key Tools and Frameworks:

- **TensorFlow.js**: TensorFlow.js is a library that allows deep learning models to run directly in the browser using JavaScript. Models can be created, trained, and even imported from TensorFlow/Keras. This library is ideal for web applications requiring interactive AI features, as it reduces latency by eliminating server calls.
- **ONNX.js**: The ONNX.js library allows ONNX models to be executed in the browser, providing cross-framework compatibility and supporting a wide range of models exported from frameworks like PyTorch and TensorFlow.
- **WebAssembly (Wasm)**: WebAssembly is a low-level binary format that enables high-performance execution in web browsers. Machine learning libraries such as Pyodide (Python in WebAssembly) and ONNX.js use WebAssembly to make web-based model inference faster and more efficient.

Benefits and Considerations:

- **Low Latency**: Data doesn't need to travel between client and server, resulting in faster predictions.
- **Offline Availability**: Client-side models can run offline, making them

suitable for environments with limited connectivity.

- **Device Limitations**: Browser-based models are limited by the user's device hardware and may perform slower on lower-end devices.

Example Use Cases:

- In-browser photo editing with real-time filters
- Gesture and facial recognition in web games
- Interactive AI-driven applications such as text autocompletion and spell-checking

2. Mobile Deployment: Bringing AI Models to Mobile Apps

Mobile deployment is essential for applications requiring on-the-go access, like personal health monitoring, augmented reality, and more. With mobile deployment, models are either run on the device itself or in the cloud, depending on the complexity of the application and hardware limitations.

A. **On-Device Deployment**

On-device deployment brings the model to the mobile device itself, which is beneficial for reducing latency and providing offline functionality. However, mobile devices have limited processing power and memory, so models must be optimized through techniques like quantization and pruning.

Key Tools and Frameworks:

- **TensorFlow Lite**: TensorFlow Lite is a lightweight version of TensorFlow optimized for mobile and embedded devices. It supports model conversion and optimization to reduce size and improve inference speed, making it suitable for applications requiring fast, on-device inference.
- **Core ML**: Core ML is Apple's machine learning framework for iOS devices. It converts and optimizes models specifically for Apple's ecosystem, enabling smooth integration with iOS features like Vision and Natural Language.

- **ONNX Runtime Mobile**: ONNX Runtime Mobile is optimized for running ONNX models on Android and iOS. It offers cross-platform support and is compatible with various model formats, allowing developers to deploy models trained on multiple frameworks.

Benefits and Considerations:

- **Offline Functionality**: On-device deployment allows models to work offline, useful for applications in remote or low-connectivity areas.
- **Low Latency**: With no need to connect to an external server, on-device models provide fast predictions.
- **Device Compatibility**: On-device models are limited by the capabilities of mobile hardware, requiring efficient model optimization.

Example Use Cases:

- Image and object recognition in augmented reality apps
- Personal assistant features like speech-to-text and natural language understanding
- Health monitoring apps that analyze real-time sensor data

B. **Cloud-Based Mobile Deployment**

In cloud-based mobile deployment, the model remains on a server, and the mobile app communicates with it through APIs. This setup is advantageous for complex models that require high computational power, which mobile devices may lack.

Key Tools and Frameworks:

- **AWS Lambda & API Gateway**: AWS Lambda enables serverless execution, so mobile apps can make HTTP requests to invoke the model. This setup is efficient and can handle high user traffic.
- **Firebase ML Kit**: Google's ML Kit provides machine learning APIs for mobile developers, making it easy to incorporate pre-trained models

for common use cases like text recognition, face detection, and image labeling.

Benefits and Considerations:

- **Access to Powerful Hardware**: The model runs on cloud servers with high-performance GPUs, enabling the use of complex models.
- **Scalability**: Cloud-based deployment can easily scale to meet high traffic demands.
- **Network Dependency**: Cloud-based models require internet connectivity, potentially introducing latency.

Example Use Cases:

- Real-time language translation in a travel app
- Visual search and object recognition for e-commerce
- Voice-controlled personal assistants

3. Best Practices for Web and Mobile Deployment

For successful deployment in web and mobile environments, consider the following best practices to ensure model performance, reliability, and user satisfaction:

- **Model Compression**: Use quantization, pruning, and knowledge distillation to reduce model size for on-device applications, balancing accuracy with resource constraints.
- **Efficient Data Handling**: For web applications, limit the amount of data transferred between client and server to reduce latency and improve user experience.
- **Caching and Pre-fetching**: Implement caching and pre-fetching techniques to improve model response time in mobile applications. Caching frequently accessed data reduces the need for redundant requests.

- **User Privacy and Security**: For models handling sensitive data, especially on mobile devices, ensure that data is securely stored and processed. Follow data protection guidelines and consider local processing when feasible.
- **Model Monitoring and Updating**: Once deployed, monitor the model's performance over time. Use feedback data to update or retrain the model periodically to improve its accuracy and adapt to changing input patterns.

Deploying deep learning models on web and mobile platforms brings AI capabilities directly to users in versatile, accessible ways. By choosing the right deployment strategy, from server-side web hosting to on-device mobile inference, developers can create fast, responsive applications that fit a range of user needs and hardware constraints. Whether for real-time image recognition, language processing, or interactive web tools, deploying AI models expands the impact of deep learning by making it available whenever and wherever users need it.

Cloud Deployment Options: Deploying Models on AWS, Google Cloud, or Azure

Cloud deployment allows deep learning models to run on powerful remote servers, offering advantages in scalability, high computational resources, and ease of access for end-users across diverse devices. By deploying models in the cloud, you can serve predictions to large numbers of users without relying on the processing power of individual devices. Here, we'll explore the main cloud platforms for AI—AWS, Google Cloud, and Microsoft Azure—focusing on the key services each platform provides for deep learning deployment.

1. AWS (Amazon Web Services)

AWS offers a comprehensive suite of tools for deploying deep learning models, making it one of the most popular platforms for cloud-based AI applications. AWS provides scalable, managed services for training, deploying, and managing machine learning models.

A. Amazon SageMaker

Amazon SageMaker is a fully managed service that simplifies every step of the machine learning workflow, including training, deploying, and monitoring models.

- **Training and Inference**: SageMaker offers Jupyter Notebook integration for building models, and it supports multiple frameworks, including TensorFlow, PyTorch, and MXNet. It handles distributed training and can automatically tune hyperparameters.

- **Endpoints for Real-Time Inference**: SageMaker allows you to deploy models as HTTP endpoints for real-time predictions. These endpoints are highly scalable and can handle large traffic loads, adapting dynamically to changes in demand.

- **Batch Transform**: For non-real-time inference, Batch Transform enables model inference on large datasets asynchronously, which is useful for processing data in bulk rather than streaming real-time requests.

- **SageMaker Studio**: SageMaker Studio provides an integrated development environment (IDE) that consolidates the entire machine learning lifecycle. It allows developers to manage datasets, run experiments, and analyze results within one interface.

B. AWS Lambda

AWS Lambda is a serverless compute service that automatically runs code in response to events, making it an ideal choice for lightweight deep learning models that don't require constant uptime.

- **Model Deployment with Lambda**: You can deploy models by packaging them as Lambda functions, which can then be triggered by events such as HTTP requests, API calls, or data uploads. This setup is cost-effective for low-demand applications, as you only pay for the compute time consumed during function execution.

- **Integrating with API Gateway**: AWS API Gateway can be used alongside Lambda to expose models as RESTful endpoints, allowing users to make predictions via HTTP requests.

C. Amazon EC2 Instances

Amazon EC2 offers customizable virtual machines that allow for flexible deployment. You can choose instances optimized for compute or memory and take advantage of high-performance GPUs to power complex models.

- **EC2 with Elastic Inference**: AWS Elastic Inference allows you to attach GPU-powered inference acceleration to EC2 instances. This setup reduces costs by only using GPU resources when needed, making it efficient for deep learning inference.

2. Google Cloud Platform (GCP)

Google Cloud Platform offers a range of AI and machine learning tools, with its TensorFlow ecosystem and BigQuery integration making it an attractive choice for data-centric AI applications.

A. AI Platform (Vertex AI)

Vertex AI, Google Cloud's fully managed machine learning platform, enables seamless end-to-end machine learning operations, from model building to deployment.

- **Training and Deployment**: Vertex AI allows you to train models on both CPU and GPU instances, and it supports AutoML for automatic model training and tuning. Deployment options include batch prediction, online prediction, and model monitoring.
- **Pre-Trained Models and AutoML**: For users who need quick solutions, Vertex AI provides AutoML services that handle model training and optimization automatically. AutoML Vision, for instance, allows developers to train custom image models without extensive coding.
- **TensorFlow Extended (TFX)**: TFX is a production-ready machine

learning pipeline tool for TensorFlow that is integrated with GCP. TFX allows you to build robust pipelines, monitor model performance, and manage data more effectively.

B. Google Kubernetes Engine (GKE)

Google Kubernetes Engine is a managed Kubernetes service that allows you to deploy containerized models in a scalable, distributed environment.

- **Serving Models with Kubernetes**: With GKE, you can deploy TensorFlow Serving containers for fast, scalable model inference. Kubernetes handles load balancing and scaling, enabling efficient management of high-demand applications.
- **Kubeflow**: Kubeflow, Google's machine learning toolkit for Kubernetes, supports end-to-end ML workflows on GKE, including data management, training, deployment, and monitoring.

C. Cloud Functions

Google Cloud Functions is a serverless environment similar to AWS Lambda. It's well-suited for deploying models that need to respond to events or handle sporadic requests.

- **Simple Model Deployment**: Cloud Functions can serve lightweight models, particularly for inference tasks that require low latency. You can also integrate Cloud Functions with Firebase for mobile and web applications.

3. Microsoft Azure

Microsoft Azure provides powerful machine learning tools, from its dedicated ML platform to containerized deployment options, making it versatile for enterprise-level AI applications.

A. Azure Machine Learning (Azure ML)

Azure ML is a comprehensive suite for machine learning that covers data preparation, model training, deployment, and monitoring.

- **Azure ML Designer**: A drag-and-drop interface in Azure ML Designer makes it easy for non-experts to build machine learning models. This tool also integrates with Jupyter Notebooks and supports Python-based training.
- **Managed Endpoints**: Azure ML's Managed Online Endpoints allow you to deploy models as RESTful services, making it simple to create production-ready APIs for real-time inference. Managed Batch Endpoints, on the other hand, are suitable for batch prediction tasks.
- **Model Registry**: Azure ML includes a model registry that helps organize multiple model versions, track metadata, and manage model deployment workflows.

B. Azure Kubernetes Service (AKS)

Azure Kubernetes Service is Microsoft's managed Kubernetes platform, ideal for deploying containerized machine learning models.

- **Scalable Deployment**: AKS integrates seamlessly with Azure ML, allowing you to deploy TensorFlow Serving or ONNX Runtime containers to provide high-performance model inference in a scalable setup. AKS manages cluster scaling and ensures optimal resource use.
- **ONNX Runtime**: Azure heavily supports the Open Neural Network Exchange (ONNX) format, which enables interoperability across AI frameworks. Models in ONNX format can be optimized and deployed for high performance using Azure's ONNX Runtime, making it especially suitable for real-time applications.

C. Azure Functions

Similar to AWS Lambda and Google Cloud Functions, Azure Functions is a serverless compute service for running lightweight models on-demand.

- **Cost-Effective Deployment**: Azure Functions allows you to create event-driven inference workflows without needing dedicated servers. This option is efficient for applications with intermittent requests, as you only pay for execution time.

4. Best Practices for Cloud Deployment

- **Model Optimization**: Before deployment, optimize your model to reduce latency and resource usage. Techniques such as quantization, pruning, and knowledge distillation are helpful for preparing models for the cloud.
- **Monitoring and Logging**: Use integrated logging and monitoring tools provided by each platform (e.g., CloudWatch on AWS, Cloud Monitoring on GCP, and Azure Monitor). Monitoring helps track model performance, detect drift, and identify potential issues.
- **Scalability**: Cloud platforms offer auto-scaling options, enabling your application to handle variable demand. Configure scaling options to ensure seamless performance during high-traffic periods.
- **Security**: Implement proper security measures, such as data encryption, user authentication, and access control. Ensure that sensitive data is protected during model deployment and inference.
- **Cost Management**: Cloud deployment can incur substantial costs if not managed properly. Use cost-saving measures like serverless computing for low-demand applications, and monitor usage patterns to identify optimization opportunities.

AWS, Google Cloud, and Microsoft Azure each offer robust, flexible options for deploying deep learning models in the cloud. Whether you need real-time inference through serverless functions or scalable containerized deployments via Kubernetes, these platforms provide the necessary tools to streamline deployment and maximize performance. By selecting the appropriate cloud services and following best practices for optimization, monitoring, and cost management, you can build a cloud-based deep learning solution that meets the needs of modern applications while reaching a wide user base.

API Integration: Building an API for Your Model Using Flask or FastAPI

Integrating a deep learning model into a web-based API enables other applications, systems, or end-users to interact with the model remotely, making it more accessible and versatile. By using a lightweight web framework like Flask or FastAPI, you can deploy your model with a RESTful API that allows clients to make HTTP requests for predictions. Here's a comprehensive guide on building an API for your model with these popular Python frameworks, covering setup, endpoint creation, and best practices.

1. Choosing Flask or FastAPI

Flask and **FastAPI** are both popular choices for deploying machine learning models as web APIs. Here's a brief comparison:

- **Flask**: Known for its simplicity and flexibility, Flask is a minimalistic framework that's straightforward to set up. It's ideal for small-to-medium projects and supports a wide range of extensions. While it lacks native asynchronous support, it's still highly effective for basic API deployment.
- **FastAPI**: Designed for high performance, FastAPI is a newer framework with native support for asynchronous programming (async/await). It's faster than Flask and better suited for handling high-demand applications. FastAPI also includes automatic request validation and documentation generation, making it an excellent choice for more complex or large-scale APIs.

Both frameworks can handle model deployments well, but if low-latency response times are a priority, FastAPI is generally preferred. For this guide, we'll provide examples using both Flask and FastAPI.

2. Setting Up Your API Project

Before building the API, ensure you have the necessary libraries installed:

```bash
bash
```

```bash
# Install Flask and/or FastAPI
pip install flask
pip install fastapi uvicorn
# Install additional dependencies for model handling
pip install tensorflow  # or PyTorch, depending on your model
```

3. Building the API with Flask

In this example, we'll create an API endpoint using Flask that loads a pre-trained model and accepts JSON input for predictions.

A. Basic API Structure in Flask
Set up the Project Structure
Organize the files as follows:

```bash
bash
```

```
my_flask_api/ ├───────
  model/ │    └───────
      model.h5        # Your pre-trained model file ├───────
  app.py              # Main API file └───────
  requirements.txt    # List of dependencies
```

Code the Flask API

```python
python
```

```python
# app.py
from flask import Flask, request, jsonify
import tensorflow as tf
import numpy as np

# Initialize the Flask app
app = Flask(__name__)
```

```
# Load the model
model = tf.keras.models.load_model("model/model.h5")

# Define the prediction endpoint
@app.route('/predict', methods=['POST'])
def predict():
    data = request.get_json(force=True)
    # Assume input data is in 'data' key of JSON request
    input_data = np.array(data['data']).reshape(1, -1)
    prediction = model.predict(input_data)
    return jsonify({'prediction': prediction.tolist()})

if __name__ == '__main__':
    app.run(debug=True, host='0.0.0.0', port=5000)
```

- **Explanation**: This code initializes a Flask application, loads the model, and sets up a /predict endpoint. The model takes input data from the request, processes it, and returns a prediction.
- **Testing**: Start the API by running python app.py. Use tools like **Postman** or **curl** to test by sending a POST request with JSON data to http://localhost:5000/predict.

4. Building the API with FastAPI

FastAPI's native support for asynchronous code and request validation can make it more efficient for large-scale applications.

Set up the Project Structure

The structure is similar to Flask:

```css
my_fastapi_api/ ├───────
  model/ │   └───────
    model.h5 ├──────
  main.py              # Main API file └──────
```

```
requirements.txt
```

Code the FastAPI API

```python
python

# main.py
from fastapi import FastAPI, HTTPException
from pydantic import BaseModel
import tensorflow as tf
import numpy as np

# Define the data structure for input
class ModelInput(BaseModel):
    data: list

# Initialize FastAPI app
app = FastAPI()

# Load the model
model = tf.keras.models.load_model("model/model.h5")

# Define the prediction endpoint
@app.post('/predict')
async def predict(input_data: ModelInput):
    data_array = np.array(input_data.data).reshape(1, -1)
    prediction = model.predict(data_array)
    return {'prediction': prediction.tolist()}
```

- **Explanation**: FastAPI's BaseModel class enables data validation, automatically checking that the request data is in the expected format.
- **Starting the API**: Run FastAPI with Uvicorn: uvicorn main:app —reload. Access the API documentation by going to http://127.0.0. 1:8000/docs.

5. Testing the API
To test your API, use a tool like Postman or the command line.

Example **curl** command:

```bash
curl -X POST "http://127.0.0.1:5000/predict" -H "Content-Type:
application/json" -d '{"data": [1, 2, 3, 4]}'
```

The response should contain a JSON object with the model's prediction.

6. Securing Your API

Add security features as needed, especially for production environments:

- **API Keys**: Require an API key to access endpoints.
- **Authentication and Authorization**: Use OAuth or JWT for secure access.
- **Rate Limiting**: Limit the number of requests per user/IP to prevent abuse.
- **Input Validation**: Validate inputs rigorously to protect against injection attacks.

7. Best Practices for Deployment

Dockerize the Application: Use Docker to create a container for your API, ensuring it runs consistently across environments.

Example Dockerfile:

```dockerfile
FROM python:3.8-slim
WORKDIR /app
COPY . /app
RUN pip install -r requirements.txt
CMD ["python", "app.py"]
```

1. **Use a Load Balancer**: For high-demand applications, a load balancer

can distribute incoming requests across multiple instances of your API.

2. **Set Up Auto-Scaling**: Deploy the API on a cloud platform with auto-scaling capabilities (e.g., AWS Elastic Beanstalk, GCP App Engine).

3. **Monitor and Log**: Implement logging to track errors, usage, and other metrics.

Integrating your deep learning model as an API with Flask or FastAPI transforms it into a flexible service that clients can access from anywhere. Flask provides simplicity and ease of use, while FastAPI offers performance and built-in data validation. By following best practices in deployment, security, and scalability, you can create a robust API for real-world applications, enabling users to leverage your model's insights in a wide array of contexts.

Monitoring and Maintaining Deployed Models: Model Performance Monitoring, Updating, and Scalability

Deploying a deep learning model is only the beginning of its lifecycle. Real-world deployment requires ongoing monitoring and maintenance to ensure the model remains effective, accurate, and scalable over time. This section covers best practices for monitoring model performance, updating models, and ensuring scalability in production environments.

1. Importance of Monitoring Deployed Models

Once deployed, a model may encounter changes in data patterns, user behavior, or system requirements. Monitoring helps you track the model's performance and detect potential issues such as:

- **Data Drift**: Changes in the input data distribution that can degrade model accuracy over time.
- **Concept Drift**: Changes in the relationship between inputs and outputs due to real-world events, new user behaviors, or other factors.
- **Latency and Scalability**: Ensuring the model responds quickly and

scales effectively under varying levels of demand.

By implementing monitoring systems, you can detect issues early and maintain model reliability.

2. Performance Metrics to Monitor

To maintain high performance, monitor a variety of metrics that capture the model's accuracy, efficiency, and usability:

- **Prediction Accuracy**: Track the model's accuracy, precision, recall, F1 score, or other relevant metrics depending on the task (e.g., classification, regression).
- **Latency**: Measure response times for predictions. Latency should stay within an acceptable range for end-users, especially in real-time applications.
- **Throughput**: Evaluate how many requests the model can handle per second, especially under peak load conditions.
- **Resource Utilization**: Monitor CPU, GPU, and memory usage to ensure the model is running efficiently and can scale when needed.
- **Error Rate**: Track error rates, including any incorrect predictions or system errors.

Setting baseline thresholds for each metric allows you to set up alerts when values deviate significantly from expected performance, indicating a need for intervention.

3. Tools for Model Monitoring

There are several tools and platforms available to streamline the monitoring process. Here are some popular choices:

- **Prometheus and Grafana**: Open-source tools that allow you to monitor model metrics in real time. Prometheus collects and stores metrics data, while Grafana visualizes it on dashboards.

- **TensorBoard**: TensorFlow's visualization tool, useful for tracking training and validation metrics over time. It also supports limited model monitoring capabilities post-deployment.
- **Amazon SageMaker Model Monitor**: AWS's built-in service for monitoring deployed models, automatically detecting data drift, outliers, and other anomalies.
- **Datadog and New Relic**: General application monitoring tools that can track model performance, latency, and error rates as part of the broader application ecosystem.

Choosing the right tools depends on your infrastructure, model complexity, and the scale of deployment.

4. Updating Models in Production

When model performance degrades or new data becomes available, updating or retraining the model is necessary. Here are some key strategies:

- **Scheduled Retraining**: Set up a schedule (e.g., weekly, monthly) for retraining the model with new data to maintain accuracy.
- **Continuous Learning Pipelines**: For models in rapidly changing environments, consider a continuous learning pipeline. This approach automatically retrains the model with newly labeled data as it arrives.
- **A/B Testing**: Before deploying an updated model, use A/B testing to compare it against the current version. This helps determine if the new model offers a measurable improvement.
- **Canary Deployment**: Deploy the new model to a small subset of users to observe its performance before a full-scale release. If successful, gradually increase the rollout.

5. Scaling Models in Production

Scaling ensures that your model can handle increasing demand without compromising performance. Here are key strategies to consider:

- **Horizontal Scaling**: Use load balancers to distribute incoming requests across multiple instances of the model. This approach is particularly useful for handling high-traffic applications.
- **Vertical Scaling**: Increase the computational resources (e.g., CPU, GPU, RAM) allocated to the model. This can improve response times for complex models or high-throughput applications but may be limited by hardware constraints.
- **Using Serverless Frameworks**: Serverless frameworks (like AWS Lambda) automatically scale resources based on demand. These frameworks are cost-effective for intermittent workloads, as you pay only for the time the model is actively serving predictions.
- **Caching Predictions**: For models with repeatable outputs (e.g., recommendations or search results), cache predictions to reduce computational load. Cache invalidation rules ensure the cache remains up-to-date.

6. Automating Monitoring and Maintenance with MLOps

MLOps (Machine Learning Operations) is a set of best practices that bring automation to model deployment, monitoring, and updating processes. Implementing MLOps can improve your model's stability and scalability.

Key MLOps practices for monitoring and maintenance include:

- **Automated Retraining Pipelines**: Set up pipelines that periodically retrain models and automatically redeploy them if they meet performance criteria.
- **Version Control for Models**: Track different versions of models and their respective training data. This ensures reproducibility and allows you to roll back to previous versions if needed.
- **Automated Monitoring and Alerts**: Configure alerting systems to notify teams when model performance drops or infrastructure issues arise.

MLOps tools like **Kubeflow**, **MLflow**, and **Airflow** provide frameworks for managing these workflows, making it easier to maintain models and handle updates at scale.

To ensure that your deployed model remains reliable and effective:

1. **Monitor continuously**: Use tools like Prometheus, Grafana, or SageMaker Model Monitor to keep an eye on critical performance metrics.
2. **Automate maintenance**: Set up retraining pipelines, A/B testing, and alerts for model degradation.
3. **Optimize scalability**: Leverage horizontal scaling, serverless deployments, and caching for high-demand applications.
4. **Adopt MLOps**: Implement MLOps frameworks for seamless integration of monitoring, retraining, and deployment processes.

Effective monitoring and maintenance will keep your model accurate, responsive, and scalable, ultimately enhancing user satisfaction and model longevity in production.

Future Trends in Deep Learning and Ethics

C utting-Edge Research Topics: Overview of Promising Research Areas like Reinforcement Learning, Meta-Learning, and Self-Supervised Learning

As deep learning evolves, groundbreaking research areas are paving the way for more versatile, adaptive, and autonomous AI systems. This section provides an in-depth look at three of the most promising areas: reinforcement learning, meta-learning, and self-supervised learning. Each of these fields pushes the boundaries of what's possible in AI, unlocking new capabilities for applications across diverse sectors like robotics, healthcare, finance, and more.

1. Reinforcement Learning (RL)

Reinforcement learning is a branch of machine learning in which an agent learns to make decisions by interacting with its environment. It's based on the principle of trial and error, where the agent receives rewards or penalties for actions, gradually improving its policy to maximize rewards. RL has shown immense promise in areas requiring sequential decision-making, control, and strategy.

Key Concepts in Reinforcement Learning

- **Agent and Environment**: The agent interacts with an environment to achieve a goal.

- **State and Action**: At any time, the environment is in a certain state, and the agent can take an action that may affect future states.
- **Rewards and Policy**: Each action results in a reward, guiding the agent to optimize a policy (a strategy for choosing actions) that maximizes cumulative rewards over time.
- **Exploration vs. Exploitation**: RL agents balance exploring new actions to discover better rewards and exploiting known actions that yield high rewards.

Applications of Reinforcement Learning

RL is widely used in gaming, robotics, finance, and autonomous systems:

- **Gaming and Strategy**: AlphaGo, developed by DeepMind, famously used RL to beat top human players in the complex game of Go. Reinforcement learning has also shown success in complex multiplayer online games where agents must adapt to other players' strategies.
- **Robotics**: RL enables robots to learn tasks like walking, grasping, and object manipulation through continuous interaction with their environment.
- **Healthcare**: RL models can optimize treatment plans by learning from patient data to recommend personalized treatment sequences over time.
- **Finance**: Portfolio management and algorithmic trading use RL to make decisions based on market states and maximize returns.

Recent Advances in RL

Recent research in RL has focused on deep reinforcement learning (combining neural networks with RL principles), multi-agent reinforcement learning (enabling multiple agents to learn collaboratively or competitively), and model-based RL (where agents use predictive models to plan actions). Advances in hardware and simulation environments have accelerated RL research, making it increasingly feasible for real-world applications.

2. Meta-Learning

Meta-learning, often referred to as "learning to learn," aims to develop models that can quickly adapt to new tasks with minimal data. Unlike traditional models, which require large datasets for training, meta-learning models generalize across multiple tasks, learning patterns that accelerate learning in new, similar tasks.

Key Concepts in Meta-Learning

- **Few-Shot and Zero-Shot Learning**: Meta-learning often focuses on few-shot learning, where a model learns from a very limited number of examples. Zero-shot learning takes it a step further, allowing the model to generalize to entirely new tasks without any labeled examples.
- **Task Distribution**: In meta-learning, models are trained on a distribution of tasks, allowing them to identify task-agnostic features that transfer to new tasks.
- **Optimization-Based Meta-Learning**: A common approach, where the model learns an optimal initialization (e.g., using the MAML algorithm), allowing it to adapt rapidly with only a few gradient updates.
- **Metric-Based Meta-Learning**: Another approach, where models learn a similarity metric to classify new examples by comparing them to a small support set.

Applications of Meta-Learning

Meta-learning is highly applicable in domains where labeled data is scarce or expensive to obtain, and rapid adaptation is crucial:

- **Personalized Medicine**: Meta-learning allows models to adapt treatment recommendations to individual patients quickly, leveraging prior knowledge from similar cases.
- **Autonomous Vehicles**: Meta-learning enables vehicles to adapt to new environments (e.g., different weather or terrain) based on limited experiences in those conditions.
- **Natural Language Processing (NLP)**: Few-shot and zero-shot learning in NLP applications enable chatbots or virtual assistants to understand

new language tasks with minimal labeled data.

- **Industrial Automation**: Robots can use meta-learning to adapt to novel tasks on factory floors by transferring knowledge from previously learned tasks, reducing downtime and training requirements.

Recent Advances in Meta-Learning

Recent research has enhanced meta-learning by introducing models that can autonomously switch between fast and slow adaptation, optimizing the balance between generalization and specificity. Transformer architectures, which excel in capturing long-range dependencies, have also contributed to improved performance in meta-learning, especially in language and vision tasks.

3. Self-Supervised Learning (SSL)

Self-supervised learning is a paradigm that leverages unlabeled data to create labels through data transformations. In SSL, models learn from the structure within the data itself, making it highly efficient for large-scale datasets where manual labeling is impractical. SSL has emerged as a transformative approach for representation learning, especially in fields like NLP and computer vision.

Key Concepts in Self-Supervised Learning

- **Pretext Tasks**: SSL models are trained on artificial tasks (pretext tasks), where the labels are generated from the data itself. Common examples include predicting missing words in a sentence (BERT's masked language modeling) or predicting the next frame in a video sequence.
- **Contrastive Learning**: This approach focuses on learning representations by comparing similar and dissimilar pairs, enabling models to recognize intrinsic data patterns.
- **Clustering and Clustering-Based SSL**: SSL can also use clustering techniques to organize data, allowing the model to identify data structures that enhance representation quality.

- **Transfer Learning**: SSL models trained on large datasets are often fine-tuned on downstream tasks, achieving state-of-the-art performance with minimal labeled data.

Applications of Self-Supervised Learning

SSL has gained widespread adoption in applications where large-scale, unlabeled data is available:

- **Natural Language Processing**: Models like BERT and GPT have popularized SSL by learning language representations from vast text corpora, achieving high performance on a range of NLP tasks.
- **Image and Video Processing**: SSL enables image classification, object detection, and video analysis with reduced dependence on labeled data, beneficial for autonomous systems and surveillance applications.
- **Medical Imaging**: In medical imaging, SSL allows models to learn from vast amounts of unlabeled scans, improving diagnostic accuracy without requiring extensive labeled datasets.
- **Speech and Audio Processing**: SSL models can learn to recognize speech patterns, music genres, and other auditory data features without labeled data, aiding in tasks like voice recognition and audio classification.

Recent Advances in Self-Supervised Learning

Innovations in SSL have led to models capable of learning from complex, high-dimensional data more efficiently. Techniques like contrastive learning (used in models like SimCLR and MoCo) have enhanced SSL's ability to create robust representations in computer vision. Additionally, multi-modal SSL models, capable of integrating information from text, images, and audio, represent the next frontier in this field.

Reinforcement learning, meta-learning, and self-supervised learning are transforming the capabilities of AI, each offering unique benefits and addressing specific challenges in deep learning.

- **Reinforcement Learning** is ideal for decision-making tasks requiring continuous interaction with an environment. It has promising applications in gaming, robotics, healthcare, and finance.
- **Meta-Learning** shines in settings where rapid adaptation to new tasks with minimal data is essential, such as personalized medicine and autonomous vehicles.
- **Self-Supervised Learning** leverages unlabeled data to learn robust representations, making it invaluable for fields with vast amounts of raw data like NLP, computer vision, and medical imaging.

The advancements in these fields signal a shift toward more adaptable, generalizable, and data-efficient deep learning models, positioning them as pivotal areas for future research and application.

AI Ethics and Responsibility: Discussing Ethical Implications, Model Biases, and Responsible AI Practices

As artificial intelligence (AI) continues to permeate every facet of society, it is crucial to examine the ethical implications of its development and deployment. The rapidly evolving field of AI, especially deep learning, presents unique challenges that demand a thoughtful, responsible approach to ensure fairness, transparency, accountability, and safety. This section will explore the ethical concerns in AI, including model biases, transparency issues, and the broader societal impacts of AI technologies. Moreover, we will highlight the importance of responsible AI practices, which are essential for building trust in AI systems.

1. Ethical Implications of AI

AI systems are becoming increasingly capable of making decisions that impact individuals' lives. From healthcare and finance to hiring practices and criminal justice, AI systems can influence significant outcomes. However, without careful consideration, AI systems can have unintended consequences, both for the individuals directly affected and society at large. Several ethical issues are central to AI development, including privacy, accountability, and the potential for harm.

Privacy and Surveillance

AI technologies, particularly those involving large-scale data collection, raise concerns about privacy. AI models rely on vast amounts of data, often sourced from individuals without their explicit consent or knowledge. For example, facial recognition technology has sparked significant privacy debates, as it enables surveillance on an unprecedented scale. The collection of sensitive data, such as health records, financial transactions, and personal preferences, can also raise questions about who owns the data and how it is used.

Accountability and Transparency

As AI models become more complex, especially with deep learning, they often operate as "black boxes"—difficult for even the developers to fully explain or interpret. This lack of transparency makes it challenging to hold systems accountable when things go wrong. For instance, in applications like autonomous driving, if a self-driving car causes an accident, who is to blame—the car's manufacturer, the AI system itself, or the human oversight? The inability to trace decisions made by AI models raises significant challenges in legal and regulatory frameworks.

Bias and Discrimination

AI models are inherently shaped by the data on which they are trained. If the data reflects historical biases, these biases can be amplified or even perpetuated by AI systems. For instance, facial recognition algorithms have shown to have higher error rates for people with darker skin tones, women, and non-Western faces, due to biases in the training data. Similarly, predictive algorithms used in hiring or criminal justice systems may perpetuate existing social inequalities, discriminating against marginalized groups.

This phenomenon is known as **algorithmic bias**, where AI models unintentionally favor one group over others due to the biases present in the data. Addressing these biases requires more than just technical fixes—it demands a holistic approach that includes ethical considerations in data collection, algorithm design, and deployment.

2. Addressing Bias in AI Models

Bias in AI models arises from multiple sources, and understanding these sources is critical in mitigating their impact. The primary sources of bias include:

- **Bias in Training Data**: If the data used to train AI models is biased, the model will reflect that bias. For example, training a model to predict job performance using historical hiring data may perpetuate gender or racial biases if the past hiring decisions were biased.
- **Sampling Bias**: This occurs when the training dataset is not representative of the population the model is intended to serve. For example, a dataset for a medical AI system may lack diversity in terms of race, gender, or age, which can result in the model performing poorly for underrepresented groups.
- **Label Bias**: In supervised learning, biases in labeling can occur when human annotators have their own prejudices or interpretations, leading to skewed training labels.
- **Model Bias**: Even with balanced datasets, certain machine learning algorithms can introduce biases through the way they process and prioritize data.

Strategies to Mitigate Bias

To address and mitigate bias in AI models, several strategies can be employed:

- **Diverse Data Collection**: Collecting data from diverse sources and ensuring it represents the population the model will serve is crucial. This involves actively seeking data that includes underrepresented groups and addressing historical biases.
- **Bias Detection and Auditing**: Regularly testing AI systems for biases, even after deployment, helps identify issues before they escalate. Techniques such as fairness metrics and adversarial testing can reveal potential discrimination in model predictions.
- **Algorithmic Fairness**: There are various fairness algorithms that aim to reduce discrimination by adjusting the way models make predictions or decisions. These algorithms aim to ensure that protected groups (e.g., gender, race, or ethnicity) are treated equitably by the model.

3. Responsible AI Practices

Responsible AI is about ensuring that AI systems are developed and deployed in a way that benefits society while minimizing harm. It is crucial for organizations to follow best practices that emphasize fairness, transparency, accountability, and security in AI development.

Fairness and Equality

AI systems should be designed to ensure that they operate in a fair and unbiased manner, providing equal opportunities and outcomes to all individuals, regardless of their demographic characteristics. This includes addressing bias in the dataset, model, and evaluation metrics. Additionally, fairness should extend to access to AI benefits—ensuring that disadvantaged groups are not excluded from the positive impacts of AI technologies.

Transparency and Explainability

As AI systems become more ubiquitous, transparency and explainability become key aspects of responsible AI. It is essential that AI models, especially in high-stakes areas like healthcare and finance, provide explanations for their decisions. This helps users understand how AI systems reach conclusions, which is crucial for trust and accountability. Transparent systems also allow developers to identify and correct issues with the model.

Explainable AI (XAI) is a growing field that focuses on making complex models, particularly deep learning systems, interpretable without compromising performance. The goal of XAI is to ensure that even sophisticated models can provide human-understandable reasoning for their predictions, which is essential for adoption in regulated fields such as healthcare or finance.

Accountability and Governance

Accountability is one of the most significant challenges in AI ethics. Establishing clear lines of responsibility for AI system outcomes is critical to ensure that there is recourse when things go wrong. This could involve holding AI developers accountable for the design and performance of their models, as well as ensuring that AI deployment aligns with ethical guidelines.

Governance frameworks are also essential in managing AI systems' lifecycle—from development and deployment to monitoring and maintenance. These frameworks define how decisions regarding AI development and deployment are made, who makes them, and how risks are mitigated.

Security and Safety

AI systems must be secure and safe from potential threats. As AI becomes more embedded in critical infrastructure, it is essential to protect these systems from malicious attacks, such as adversarial attacks, where small changes to input data can cause the model to make incorrect predictions. Ensuring the safety of AI systems also involves making sure that they are robust and fail gracefully in situations where they encounter unexpected or incorrect data.

Ethical Guidelines and Regulations

AI ethics is an evolving field, and various organizations are establishing ethical guidelines and regulations to ensure responsible AI use. These frameworks, such as the **EU's Ethical Guidelines for Trustworthy AI**, emphasize respect for human rights, non-discrimination, and the importance of transparency and accountability. Governments, industry leaders, and research organizations must collaborate to create policies that balance the development of AI with ethical considerations.

4. The Role of AI Practitioners in Ethics

AI practitioners, including data scientists, machine learning engineers, and researchers, must take responsibility for the ethical implications of their work. This responsibility goes beyond simply creating functional models—it extends to considering the societal impact of the technologies they develop. Ethical AI practitioners should:

- Engage in continuous learning about ethical issues and incorporate these principles into their workflows.
- Participate in interdisciplinary collaboration with ethicists, sociologists, and legal experts to better understand the broader implications of their work.
- Advocate for the adoption of ethical guidelines and fairness protocols within their organizations and industries.

As AI technologies, particularly deep learning, become more sophisticated, the ethical concerns surrounding them will continue to grow in importance. Addressing issues like model bias, privacy, and transparency, while promoting fairness, accountability, and security, is essential for fostering trust and ensuring that AI serves the broader public good. Responsible AI development requires continuous effort from researchers, developers, organizations, and regulators to create systems that are not only intelligent but also ethical and aligned with societal values.

Where to Go Next: Resources for Advanced Study, Ongoing Research, and Professional Development in Deep Learning

As deep learning continues to evolve, it opens up numerous possibilities for researchers, practitioners, and enthusiasts to delve deeper into the field. Whether you're looking to advance your knowledge, stay current with the latest developments, or embark on a career in deep learning, there are a wealth of resources available. This section will guide you through various pathways for further learning, exploration, and professional development in deep learning.

1. Online Courses and MOOCs

The best way to continue your deep learning journey is by enrolling in specialized online courses that dive deeper into advanced topics. Many well-regarded platforms provide structured, hands-on learning experiences, including:

- **Coursera**:
- *Deep Learning Specialization by Andrew Ng* (offered by Deeplearning.ai)
- *AI for Everyone* (by Andrew Ng)
- *Convolutional Neural Networks for Visual Recognition* (Stanford University)
- **edX**:
- *Deep Learning with Python and Keras* (offered by Microsoft)
- *Advanced Machine Learning Specialization* (offered by the National Research University Higher School of Economics)
- **Udacity**:
- *AI Programming with Python Nanodegree*
- *Deep Learning Nanodegree* (for hands-on model-building experience)

These courses provide both theoretical insights and practical applications, enabling learners to develop real-world deep learning skills.

2. Books for Advanced Study

While online resources and courses are excellent, books remain an invaluable resource for deep, theoretical insights. Some advanced books that can expand your understanding include:

- **"Deep Learning" by Ian Goodfellow, Yoshua Bengio, and Aaron Courville**: Often considered the bible of deep learning, this book provides a thorough grounding in the mathematical and conceptual aspects of deep learning.
- **"Hands-On Machine Learning with Scikit-Learn, Keras, and TensorFlow" by Aurélien Géron**: A great resource for practical implementations, especially with TensorFlow and Keras, this book walks you through various algorithms, tools, and techniques in deep learning.
- **"Deep Reinforcement Learning Hands-On" by Maxim Lapan**: If you're looking to explore reinforcement learning in depth, this book provides hands-on examples and practical guides.
- **"Bayesian Reasoning and Machine Learning" by David Barber**: This is an excellent book for those interested in the probabilistic aspects of deep learning and machine learning in general.

3. Research Papers and Journals

The most cutting-edge developments in deep learning come from academic research, so keeping up with the latest papers is essential for anyone aiming to stay at the forefront of the field. Some of the leading journals and conferences in deep learning research include:

- **Journals**:
- *Journal of Machine Learning Research (JMLR)*
- *IEEE Transactions on Neural Networks and Learning Systems*
- *Pattern Recognition* (Elsevier)
- *Nature Machine Intelligence*
- **Conferences**:
- *NeurIPS (Conference on Neural Information Processing Systems)*: A premier conference for deep learning and artificial intelligence research.
- *ICML (International Conference on Machine Learning)*: One of the largest conferences in machine learning, with numerous papers on deep learning innovations.

- *CVPR (Computer Vision and Pattern Recognition Conference)*: Focused on deep learning applications in computer vision.
- *ICLR (International Conference on Learning Representations)*: A highly influential conference in the deep learning community.
- *AAAI (Association for the Advancement of Artificial Intelligence)*: An annual conference with a wide range of topics related to AI and deep learning.

By reading the latest papers from these conferences and journals, you can stay updated on breakthroughs in neural network architectures, optimization techniques, and more.

4. Research Platforms and Communities

Engaging with the broader deep learning research community can significantly enhance your understanding of the field. Here are some platforms where you can find research papers, open-source projects, and collaborate with other professionals:

- **ArXiv**: A free distribution service and an open-access archive for scholarly articles in the fields of physics, mathematics, computer science, quantitative biology, and more. Many of the latest deep learning papers are published here before they appear in journals.
- **Google Scholar**: A freely accessible web search engine that indexes scholarly articles across various disciplines. You can use it to find research papers, theses, books, and conference proceedings on deep learning topics.
- **GitHub**: A platform for code sharing and collaboration. Many deep learning researchers and developers post their code and models on GitHub, making it a valuable resource for learning by example. You can explore repositories, contribute to projects, and even start your own.
- **Kaggle**: A data science and machine learning community that offers datasets, competitions, and collaboration opportunities. Kaggle also has tutorials and an active community where you can learn from experienced practitioners.

- **Stack Overflow and Reddit**: Platforms like Stack Overflow and Reddit's r/MachineLearning community offer spaces to ask questions, share insights, and stay updated on the latest trends.

5. Master's and Ph.D. Programs

For those who are deeply committed to the field and wish to pursue it at the highest level, a formal academic program may be the right step. Several prestigious institutions offer advanced degrees in AI and deep learning, including:

- **Stanford University**: Offers both graduate and post-graduate programs in AI and machine learning, with research labs dedicated to deep learning and neural networks.
- **Massachusetts Institute of Technology (MIT)**: MIT's Department of Electrical Engineering and Computer Science (EECS) offers advanced courses and programs with a strong focus on deep learning research.
- **Carnegie Mellon University**: Known for its AI research, CMU offers a range of programs and research opportunities in deep learning and AI.
- **University of California, Berkeley**: UC Berkeley offers an AI and machine learning master's program with a heavy emphasis on deep learning, alongside dedicated research labs.

A master's or Ph.D. in AI, machine learning, or a related field allows you to develop advanced skills and engage in cutting-edge research. This path provides an opportunity to contribute to the scientific community, shaping the future of deep learning.

6. Professional Certifications and Development

For professionals who want to demonstrate their expertise in deep learning, obtaining certifications can be an effective way to advance their careers. Some of the most recognized certifications in deep learning and AI include:

- **Google's TensorFlow Certification**: This certification is ideal for those looking to demonstrate their deep learning skills using Tensor-Flow. It covers model building, training, and deployment.
- **Deep Learning Specialization by Andrew Ng on Coursera**: This specialization, offered by Deeplearning.ai, covers a wide range of deep learning topics, and completing it earns you a certificate that is recognized in the industry.
- **Microsoft Certified: Azure AI Engineer Associate**: This certification validates your skills in deploying AI solutions using Azure, with a focus on deep learning.
- **Udacity AI and Deep Learning Nanodegrees**: Udacity offers a variety of nanodegrees focused on AI and deep learning. These include hands-on projects and mentorship to guide you through advanced deep learning concepts.

7. Staying Updated with Industry Trends

In addition to formal study and research, it is important to keep up with the latest industry trends. Some of the best ways to stay informed include:

- **AI and Deep Learning Blogs**:
- *Distill.pub*: A journal dedicated to clear and elegant explanations of machine learning concepts.
- *The Machine Learning Mastery blog* by Jason Brownlee: Provides tutorials, case studies, and in-depth explanations of machine learning techniques.
- *TensorFlow Blog*: Offers updates on new features, applications, and real-world uses of TensorFlow.
- **AI Podcasts and Webinars**: Listening to AI-focused podcasts such as *The TWIML AI Podcast* or *AI Alignment Podcast* can provide insights into the latest research and practical applications of deep learning.
- **Meetups and Conferences**: Joining AI and deep learning meetups in your area or attending global conferences (like NeurIPS or ICML) can provide opportunities to network with other professionals and stay updated on the latest trends and technologies.

Deep learning is a rapidly evolving field with an abundance of resources available for those wishing to deepen their expertise. Whether you pursue advanced academic study, continue through self-directed learning with books and online courses, or engage with the research community, there are multiple paths to mastering deep learning. By continuously updating your knowledge, developing practical skills, and contributing to ongoing research, you can stay ahead in this dynamic and exciting field.